STOP WARS

KEEPING THE PEACE

CONTENTS

Stop Wars: Keeping the Peace":

PART 1: UNDERSTANDING CONFLICT

CHAPTER 1: INTRODUCTION TO CONFLICT

In a world marred by turmoil and unrest, the concept of conflict has become an all-too-familiar presence. At its core, conflict can be defined as a clash of interests, ideas, or values that leads to disagreement and tension. Throughout history, humanity has grappled with various forms of conflict, ranging from personal disputes to large-scale wars that engulf entire nations.

Conflicts come in diverse manifestations, each with its unique set of complexities. Interpersonal conflicts, for instance, arise in our daily lives when individuals have differing perspectives or desires. On a broader scale, conflicts may emerge within the borders of a single state, leading to intra-state conflicts characterized by political struggles, ethnic tensions, or economic disparities. Inter-state conflicts, on the other hand, involve disputes between different nations, often resulting from territorial ambitions, ideological differences, or historical grievances.

The causes of conflicts are multi-faceted, often stemming from a combination of factors. Historical animosities between groups can fuel long-standing conflicts, with deep-rooted resentments passed down through generations. Political power struggles and the quest for dominance can also ignite conflicts as competing factions vie for control and influence. Socio-economic disparities and inequality can breed discontent and lead to social unrest, contributing to the emergence of conflicts.

The impact of conflicts extends far beyond the individuals directly involved, leaving lasting scars on societies and nations. In regions plagued by protracted conflicts, infrastructure is destroyed, economies collapse, and communities are torn apart. The human toll is immeasurable, with lives lost or forever altered, leaving behind grief, trauma, and displacement. Furthermore, conflicts can hinder development and disrupt humanitarian efforts, making it challenging to provide aid and support to those in need.

The Psychology of Conflict

To effectively address conflicts and work towards sustainable peace, it is crucial to understand the psychology behind human behaviour in such circumstances. Conflict often triggers powerful emotions, such as fear, anger, and distrust, which can cloud judgment and escalate tensions. In the heat of the moment, individuals may resort to violence or aggressive behaviour, seeking to protect their interests or assert their dominance.

Perceptions and misperceptions play a significant role in fuelling conflicts. Different parties involved in a dispute may hold contrasting views of the same situation, leading to misunderstandings and further discord. Stereotypes and prejudices can exacerbate conflicts, as people view others through biased lenses, deepening divisions and preventing meaningful dialogue.

Communication, or the lack thereof, is another critical factor in the escalation or resolution of conflicts. Poor communication can lead to misunderstandings, as parties fail to articulate their concerns or listen to each other's perspectives. Effective communication, on the other hand, can foster empathy, facilitate compromise, and pave the way for peaceful resolutions.

Conflict Resolution Strategies

In the quest to stop wars and maintain peace, conflict resolution strategies are essential tools. There are various approaches to conflict resolution, each tailored to the specific nature of the conflict at hand. Negotiation is a widely used method, wherein parties come together to discuss their interests and reach a mutually acceptable agreement. Mediation involves the intervention of a neutral third party who helps facilitate communication and compromise between conflicting parties.

In some cases, reconciliation and forgiveness are instrumental in healing wounds and moving towards peace. Truth and reconciliation processes, for instance, allow communities to confront past atrocities, acknowledge wrongdoing, and seek forgiveness. Such initiatives can foster understanding, bridge divides, and pave the way for peaceful coexistence.

The Role of International Organizations in Peacekeeping

As conflicts often transcend national borders, the involvement of international organizations in peacekeeping efforts is crucial. The United Nations (UN) is a prominent example of a global organization dedicated to maintaining international peace and security. Through peacekeeping missions, the UN deploys personnel and resources to conflict zones, working to stabilize situations, protect civilians, and facilitate the peaceful resolution of disputes.

Other regional organizations, such as the African Union (AU) and the European Union (EU), also play significant roles in peacekeeping and conflict resolution within their respective areas of influence. These organizations often collaborate with the UN and other partners to address conflicts and promote stability.

Preventing Conflict: Diplomacy and Dialogue

One of the most effective ways to stop wars is to prevent conflicts from arising in the first place. Diplomacy and dialogue are essential tools in conflict prevention, allowing parties to engage in constructive discussions and find peaceful solutions to their differences.

Preventive diplomacy involves early intervention by third parties, such as governments or international organizations, to address potential sources of conflict and defuse tensions before they escalate. By identifying and addressing root causes of conflict, preventive diplomacy seeks to create an environment conducive to peaceful coexistence.

Furthermore, fostering dialogue and promoting understanding between different communities and nations is critical in preventing conflicts. Initiatives that promote cultural exchange, educational programs that encourage diversity and tolerance, and diplomatic efforts that encourage open communication can all contribute to conflict prevention and peacebuilding.

Conclusion: A World of Peace

In a world grappling with various conflicts, achieving lasting peace may seem like an elusive goal. However, history has shown that through concerted efforts, compassion, and understanding, it is possible to make significant strides towards a more peaceful world.

The journey to stop wars and keep the peace begins with acknowledging the complexities of conflicts and their impact on individuals and societies. Understanding the psychological aspects of conflict allows us to navigate through emotions and biases, fostering empathy and open communication between conflicting parties.

Conflict resolution strategies offer paths to finding common ground and building bridges between adversaries. Negotiation, mediation, and reconciliation provide opportunities for parties to work towards peaceful resolutions and healing.

International organizations, such as the United Nations and regional bodies, play vital roles in peacekeeping and conflict prevention. Their collective efforts demonstrate the power of global collaboration in addressing conflicts and fostering stability.

However, preventing conflicts before they escalate is equally crucial. Diplomacy and dialogue pave the way for peaceful resolutions, enabling societies to address underlying issues and seek common ground.

In the pursuit of a peaceful world, individual

actions matter as well. Each person has the power to promote understanding, embrace diversity, and reject violence. By championing empathy, tolerance, and compassion in our daily interactions, we can contribute to the fabric of peace that binds us all.

The journey towards a world of peace may be fraught with challenges, setbacks, and obstacles. Yet, history has shown that the indomitable spirit of humanity can overcome even the darkest of times.

As we look to the future, let us remember the lessons learned from past conflicts and the resilience displayed by those who have dared to dream of a better world. The legacy of those who have worked tirelessly for peace serves as a beacon, guiding us forward.

The path to peace is not a linear one; it requires continuous effort, unwavering commitment, and an enduring belief in the possibility of change. It may take generations, but if we strive for unity, understanding, and justice, we move closer to the dream of a world free from the horrors of war.

In the end, it is not only about stopping wars; it is about building a world where peace is cherished, nurtured, and protected. It is about acknowledging our shared humanity and the interconnectedness of all living beings.

Together, hand in hand, we can create a world where conflicts are resolved through dialogue, differences are celebrated, and diversity is embraced. It is a world where compassion, empathy, and understanding are our guiding principles, leading us towards a brighter and more harmonious future.

As we reflect on the journey to stop wars and keep the peace, let us remember that the power to change the world lies within each one of us. We are the architects of our destiny, and by choosing to love over hate, understanding over ignorance, and peace over violence, we can pave the way for a world where wars are but a distant memory.

In the end, the dream of a world at peace is not just a possibility; it is a necessity. It is our shared responsibility to work towards this dream, to protect the fragile fabric of peace that binds us, and to leave behind a legacy of hope for future generations.

So, let us march forward, hand in hand, towards the horizon of peace, where conflicts are but a whisper in the wind and the dreams of a harmonious world become a reality. For in the journey to stop wars and keep the peace, we discover the true essence of our humanity and the limitless potential of our collective spirit.

CHAPTER 2: CONFLICT RESOLUTION THEORIES

In the pursuit of a more peaceful world, understanding the theories and methods of conflict resolution becomes paramount. Conflict, inherent in human nature, has shaped the course of history, leaving behind tales of destruction and suffering. However, within these stories, we find glimmers of hope and evidence of humanity's capacity to resolve differences peacefully.

At the heart of conflict resolution lies the recognition that conflicts can be addressed in various ways, and the outcomes can profoundly impact individuals, communities, and nations. As we delve into the theories that underpin conflict resolution, we open the door to transformative possibilities and a world where wars are but a distant memory.

**Overview of Conflict Resolution Theories: **

Conflict resolution theories offer insights into the fundamental approaches used to manage and resolve conflicts. From win-lose scenarios to collaborative win-win solutions, each theory reflects different philosophies and strategies.

The win-lose approach, also known as the adversarial or competitive model, sees conflicts as zero-sum games where one party's gain comes at the expense of the other. In contrast, the win-win approach focuses on finding solutions that benefit all parties involved, recognizing the potential for mutual gains.

Another essential conflict resolution theory is principled negotiation, popularized by the book "Getting to Yes" by Roger Fisher and William Ury. This theory emphasizes the separation of people from the problem, focusing on interests rather than positions, and generating options for mutual gain.

**The Role of Communication in Resolving Conflicts: **

Effective communication forms the cornerstone of conflict resolution. Miscommunication and misunderstandings often escalate conflicts, while open and honest dialogue can lead to understanding and resolution.

Active listening is a critical aspect of communication in conflict resolution. When parties feel heard and acknowledged, they are more likely to engage constructively. Empathy, compassion, and respect create a fertile ground for resolving conflicts peacefully.

**Mediation, Negotiation, and Arbitration: **

Various methods exist to resolve conflicts, and the choice of approach depends on the nature and complexity of the conflict. Mediation involves a neutral third-party facilitating communication and negotiation between conflicting parties. The mediator helps parties explore solutions and reach mutually satisfactory agreements.

Negotiation is a process where conflicting parties engage directly to find common ground and reach compromises. Negotiators employ various strategies to create opportunities for resolution and avoid confrontations.

Arbitration, on the other hand, involves submitting the conflict to a neutral third party who renders a binding decision after hearing both sides' arguments.

**Case Studies of Successful Conflict Resolution Efforts: **

Throughout history, there have been remarkable instances of successful conflict resolution efforts.

The end of apartheid in South Africa is a prominent example, where negotiation and reconciliation paved the way for a new era of democracy and equality.

Additionally, the peace agreements in Northern Ireland, ending decades of sectarian violence, demonstrated the power of dialogue and compromise in resolving deeply entrenched conflicts.

These case studies serve as beacons of hope, illustrating the transformative potential of conflict resolution theories in fostering peace and stability.

In exploring conflict resolution theories and practices, we realize that there is no one-size-fits-all approach to stopping wars and keeping the peace. Each conflict is unique, influenced by historical, cultural, and political contexts. As such, the path to resolution may require creativity, patience, and resilience.

Nevertheless, armed with knowledge and a commitment to building a more peaceful world, conflict resolution becomes an indispensable tool in our collective journey to transcend the horrors of war and embrace the possibilities of peace.

In the next chapters, we will delve deeper into the practical applications of conflict resolution theories, examining real-world scenarios where these methods have made a difference. By equipping ourselves with the wisdom of the past and the tools of the present, we can begin to forge a brighter future, where conflicts are resolved with compassion, understanding, and a shared vision for a world at peace.

PART 2: THE IMPORTANCE OF PEACE

CHAPTER 3: UNDERSTANDIN G PEACE

Peace, a timeless aspiration of humanity, is more than just the absence of conflict; it is a state of harmonious coexistence and mutual understanding among individuals, communities, and nations. In this chapter, we embark on a journey to understand the essence of peace and its transformative power in shaping a more compassionate and prosperous world.

**Definition of Peace: **

Peace is a multifaceted concept that encompasses both inner tranquillity and outer harmony. At its core, peace signifies a state of calmness and non-violence, where individuals live in harmony with one another and their surroundings. It is a state of equilibrium, where conflicts are resolved peacefully, and respect for diversity is nurtured.

**Different Dimensions of Peace: **

Peace can be categorized into various dimensions, each contributing to the overall fabric of harmonious coexistence. Negative peace refers to the absence of direct violence, such as wars and armed conflicts. However, negative peace does not address the root causes of conflict and may leave underlying tensions unresolved.

Positive peace, on the other hand, delves into the creation of a just and equitable society where social, economic, and political structures promote well-being and inclusivity. Positive peace seeks to address the root causes of conflict, fostering sustainable peace and preventing future violence.

**The Significance of Peace for Individual Well-Being and Societal Progress: **

Peace plays a fundamental role in enhancing individual well-being and mental health. In peaceful environments, people can flourish, cultivate meaningful relationships, and pursue personal growth and fulfilment. The absence of fear and violence allows individuals to focus on education, creativity, and personal development.

Moreover, peace is a catalyst for societal progress and prosperity. Nations at peace are better equipped to allocate resources towards education, healthcare, and infrastructure, laying the foundation for sustainable development and equitable prosperity.

**Peace as a Foundation for Sustainable Development: **

Sustainable development, a vision of progress that meets the needs of the present without compromising the ability of future generations to meet their own needs, is inseparable from peace. In regions torn apart by conflict, development efforts are hampered, leaving communities trapped in cycles of poverty and instability.

Peace provides the fertile ground upon which sustainable development can flourish. In peaceful societies, resources can be channelled towards addressing socio-economic disparities, improving access to education and healthcare, and fostering innovation and creativity.

**The Role of Education in Fostering Peace: **

Education emerges as a potent tool in cultivating a culture of peace. By instilling values of empathy, tolerance, and conflict resolution in future generations, education becomes an agent of change, empowering individuals to become advocates for peace in their communities and beyond.

**Promoting Peaceful Coexistence in a Globalized World: **

In an increasingly interconnected and globalized world, peace takes on a global dimension.

International cooperation and diplomacy become vital in addressing transnational challenges, such as climate change, terrorism, and pandemics.

Nations must work together to create a shared vision of peace and collaborate on solutions that transcend borders. Peaceful coexistence on a global scale is not only an aspiration but a necessity for the survival and well-being of humanity.

In conclusion, understanding peace requires us to look beyond the absence of conflict and explore its multifaceted dimensions. It is not a passive state but an active pursuit, demanding collective efforts to address the root causes of violence and build just, equitable, and compassionate societies.

Peace is the foundation upon which individuals can thrive, societies can progress, and humanity can flourish. By embracing the transformative power of peace, we take the first step towards a world where wars are replaced by understanding, conflicts by dialogue, and fear by hope.

CHAPTER 4: PEACE AND HUMAN RIGHTS

Peace and human rights are inextricably intertwined, forming a symbiotic relationship that underpins the fabric of harmonious societies. In this chapter, we delve into the profound connection between peace and human rights, understanding how the protection and promotion of human rights play a pivotal role in preventing conflicts and fostering lasting peace.

**The Connection Between Peace and Human Rights: **

Human rights, as enshrined in international law and conventions, encompass the inherent dignity and equal worth of every individual. The protection of human rights is not only a moral imperative but also a fundamental prerequisite for building and maintaining peace.

In peaceful societies, individuals are granted

the freedom to express their beliefs, opinions, and identities without fear of persecution or discrimination. Respect for human rights nurtures an environment of tolerance, inclusion, and social cohesion, essential elements for peaceful coexistence.

Conversely, in societies where human rights are routinely violated, grievances and resentment can fester, leading to social unrest and conflicts. The denial of basic human rights can sow the seeds of discontent and give rise to movements seeking justice and equality, often through violent means.

**The Role of Human Rights in Preventing Conflicts: **

Human rights violations are frequently at the root of conflicts, both at the interpersonal and international levels. Injustice, discrimination, and repression can trigger anger and resistance, sparking tensions that can escalate into violence.

By upholding human rights principles, governments and institutions can address grievances and resolve conflicts through peaceful means. Respect for human rights fosters a sense of justice, enabling individuals and communities to seek redress for their grievances through nonviolent channels.

Furthermore, the protection of human rights can act as a safeguard against abuses of power and tyranny. When individuals are granted the right to participate in the decision-making processes that affect their lives, they are less likely to resort to violence to express their dissent.

**Case Studies of Conflicts Arising from Human Rights Violations: **

Throughout history, numerous conflicts have been rooted in human rights violations, serving as stark reminders of the urgent need to protect and promote human rights to preserve peace.

One such example is the Rwandan genocide in 1994, where long-standing ethnic tensions and discrimination against the Tutsi minority culminated in a horrific mass slaughter. The denial of human rights and the lack of intervention to prevent violence led to one of the darkest chapters in human history.

Similarly, the Israeli-Palestinian conflict has its origins in competing claims to land, resources, and self-determination. The violation of human rights on both sides has perpetuated a cycle of violence and deepened divisions, making the path to peace seem elusive.

These case studies serve as powerful reminders of the consequences of neglecting human rights and the urgency of addressing root causes of conflicts.

In conclusion, the preservation of peace and the protection of human rights are two sides of the same coin. Peace cannot be sustained without upholding the rights and dignity of individuals, and the promotion of human rights is a critical means of preventing conflicts.

As we strive to stop wars and keep the peace, we must recognize that human rights are not a luxury but a fundamental necessity for the well-being and security of all. Embracing human rights principles and working towards a world where every individual's rights are respected and protected is the path to a more just, equitable, and peaceful future.

CHAPTER 5: THE COST OF WAR

War, in all its devastation and horror, exacts a heavy toll on societies, leaving scars that endure long after the guns fall silent. In this chapter, we explore the multifaceted cost of war, delving into its economic, social, and environmental impact, as well as the lasting effects it inflicts on various sectors of society.

**The Economic Cost of War: **

Wars drain a nation's resources, diverting funds away from essential sectors such as education, healthcare, and infrastructure. The immense costs of maintaining armed forces, purchasing weapons, and conducting military operations strain national budgets, leaving fewer resources available for critical social programs.

Moreover, the destruction of infrastructure during wars compounds the economic burden. Roads, bridges, schools, hospitals, and other vital facilities are often targeted or collateral damage in conflicts. Rebuilding these structures is costly and time-consuming, hindering economic growth and development.

The toll on the workforce is also significant, as war often disrupts trade, agriculture, and industry. The loss of livelihoods and productivity further impedes economic progress, leading to a cycle of poverty and dependence on humanitarian aid.

**The Social Cost of War: **

War tears at the social fabric of communities, resulting in profound and far-reaching consequences. The loss of lives, particularly among the young and able-bodied, deprives societies of their most valuable human capital. Families are shattered, leaving countless children orphaned and vulnerable.

The trauma and psychological scars left by war endure for generations. Post-traumatic stress disorder (PTSD), anxiety, depression, and other mental health issues plague survivors and combatants alike. Healing from such deep emotional wounds is a slow and arduous process that hinders the rebuilding of communities.

In addition, war often leads to mass displacement, with countless individuals forced to flee their homes in search of safety. This displacement fuels refugee crises, placing additional burdens on host countries and causing further social and political tensions.

**The Environmental Cost of War: **

The impact of war on the environment is often overlooked but equally significant. Armed conflicts can result in the destruction of natural habitats, water sources, and ecosystems. Deforestation, pollution, and the use of chemical weapons lead to irreparable damage to the environment, threatening biodiversity, and long-term ecological stability.

Environmental degradation also exacerbates resource scarcity, sparking conflicts over access to water, land, and other essential resources. The competition for scarce resources can perpetuate cycles of violence and hinder efforts at peacebuilding and reconciliation.

**The Long-Term Effects of War on Societies: **

Perhaps one of the most insidious costs of war is its lasting effects on societies. War can breed hatred, mistrust, and a cycle of revenge, fuelling future conflicts. The wounds of war can linger for generations, as grievances and trauma are passed down from one generation to the next.

The breakdown of social cohesion and trust impedes post-war reconstruction and hinders efforts to build stable and inclusive societies. Rebuilding trust between communities and reconciling conflicting narratives are essential for healing and forging a path towards lasting peace.

In conclusion, the cost of war is immeasurable, encompassing not only the immediate loss of lives and destruction but also far-reaching economic, social, and environmental consequences. As we seek ways to stop wars and keep the peace, we must confront the true cost of conflict and work tirelessly to prevent the outbreak of violence. Emphasizing diplomacy, conflict resolution, and the protection of human rights can help create a world where the devastating cost of war is replaced with the enduring promise of peace and prosperity for all.

PART 3: DIPLOMACY AND INTERNATIONAL RELATIONS

CHAPTER 6: THE ROLE OF DIPLOMACY IN CONFLICT RESOLUTION

In the pursuit of peace and conflict resolution, diplomacy emerges as a powerful tool to navigate the complexities of international relations and bridge the divides between warring factions. This chapter delves into the principles and practice of diplomatic negotiation, the crucial role of diplomats and mediators, and historical examples of both diplomatic successes and challenges.

**The Principles and Practice of Diplomatic Negotiation: **

Diplomatic negotiation is an art that requires tact, skill, and an unwavering commitment to finding common ground. At its core, diplomatic negotiation seeks to promote dialogue, understanding, and compromise between conflicting parties.

One fundamental principle of diplomatic negotiation is the recognition of the parties' legitimate interests and grievances. By acknowledging the concerns of all involved, diplomats can establish an atmosphere of mutual respect and foster an environment conducive to finding solutions.

Transparency and open communication are paramount in diplomatic negotiations. Trust between parties is built through honest dialogue, which lays the foundation for durable agreements.

Moreover, diplomats often engage in shuttle diplomacy, shuttling between different parties to facilitate communication and build bridges. This approach helps to keep lines of communication open and enables negotiators to explore creative solutions that address the core issues of the conflict.

**The Role of Diplomats and Mediators in Resolving Conflicts: **

Diplomats and mediators play a pivotal role in conflict resolution, acting as neutral facilitators who bring conflicting parties to the negotiating table. Their expertise lies in understanding the nuances of the conflict, identifying common ground, and working towards consensus.

One crucial skill of diplomats and mediators is active listening. By attentively listening to the concerns and perspectives of all parties, they can uncover underlying interests and work towards mutually acceptable outcomes.

Neutrality is essential in the role of diplomats and mediators. Remaining impartial allows them to gain the trust of all parties involved, ensuring that negotiations are conducted in good faith.

In complex and protracted conflicts, mediators often employ the "step-by-step" approach, gradually addressing issues of contention in a structured manner. This approach builds momentum towards peace and helps parties gain confidence in the negotiation process.

**Diplomatic Successes and Challenges in History: **

Throughout history, diplomatic efforts have yielded both notable successes and daunting challenges in resolving conflicts.

One iconic example of successful diplomacy is the Camp David Accords in 1978, where U.S. President Jimmy Carter mediated a peace agreement between Israel and Egypt. The negotiations resulted in the first peace treaty between Israel and an Arab state, setting a precedent for future diplomatic achievements in the Middle East.

Conversely, some conflicts have proven highly resistant to diplomatic resolution. The Israeli-Palestinian conflict, for instance, has defied decades of diplomatic efforts to achieve lasting peace and security for both parties.

In recent years, cyberwarfare and disinformation campaigns have posed new challenges to traditional diplomatic negotiation. These non-traditional threats demand innovative approaches and diplomatic strategies tailored to the digital age.

**Conclusion: **

Diplomacy serves as an essential instrument in the pursuit of peace and conflict resolution. By upholding the principles of respect, transparency, and neutrality, diplomats and mediators create opportunities for dialogue and understanding between adversaries.

While diplomatic successes demonstrate the potential for peaceful resolutions, history also highlights the complexities and challenges of resolving conflicts through diplomacy. Nevertheless, the commitment to diplomatic negotiation remains vital in the collective effort to stop wars and keep the peace, paving the way for a more harmonious and secure world.

CHAPTER 7: INTERNATIONAL ORGANIZATIONS AND PEACEKEEPING

In the pursuit of global peace and conflict resolution, international organizations have emerged as critical players in maintaining stability and preventing wars. This chapter explores the role of international organizations dedicated to peacekeeping, their functions, and the challenges they face in their noble mission.

**Overview of International Organizations Dedicated to Peacekeeping: **

At the forefront of global efforts to keep the peace are international organizations like the United Nations (UN) and the North Atlantic Treaty Organization (NATO).

The United Nations, established in 1945, is a central pillar of international cooperation. Its primary purpose is to maintain international peace and security. The UN deploys peacekeeping missions to conflict zones worldwide, with the goal of creating conditions conducive to peaceful resolutions.

NATO, on the other hand, is a political and military alliance comprising 30 member countries. While NATO's primary objective is collective defence, it also plays a significant role in crisis management and peacekeeping operations.

**The Functions and Operations of Peacekeeping Missions: **

Peacekeeping missions operate under the principles of impartiality, consent of the parties involved, and non-use of force, except in self-defence. These missions are deployed to areas where armed conflicts have occurred or where there is a risk of hostilities breaking out.

The functions of peacekeeping missions vary depending on the nature of the conflict and the needs of the affected region. Some common functions include:

1. **Conflict Prevention: ** By deploying peacekeeping forces to volatile regions, international organizations can deter potential aggressors and prevent the escalation of conflicts.

2. **Disarmament and Demobilization: ** Peacekeepers often facilitate the disarmament and demobilization of combatants to promote stability and reduce the risk of renewed violence.

3. **Protection of Civilians: ** One of the essential roles of peacekeeping missions is to protect civilians caught in the crossfire of conflicts, providing safe havens and humanitarian aid.

4. **Supporting Peace Processes: ** Peacekeepers assist in implementing peace agreements and supporting political transitions, fostering conditions for lasting peace.

**The Challenges Faced by Peacekeeping Forces: **

Peacekeeping missions encounter numerous challenges that can hinder their effectiveness in maintaining peace and stability.

1. **Lack of Resources: ** Peacekeeping operations require substantial resources, including manpower, financial support, and logistical capabilities. Securing adequate resources from member countries can be challenging.

2. **Security Risks: ** Peacekeepers often operate in dangerous and volatile environments, exposing them to security risks and potential attacks by armed groups.

3. **Political Complexities: ** Peacekeeping

missions must navigate complex political landscapes, where conflicting interests among parties can hinder progress.

4. **Neutrality and Impartiality: ** Maintaining impartiality while upholding peace and security can be a delicate balancing act for peacekeepers.

**Conclusion: **

International organizations and peacekeeping missions play a vital role in preventing wars and maintaining peace in regions plagued by conflicts. By deploying neutral and capable forces, these organizations create an environment conducive to dialogue and peaceful resolutions. However, they face challenges, from resource constraints to navigating complex political landscapes. To improve the effectiveness of peacekeeping, international cooperation, adequate funding, and ongoing evaluation and adaptation of strategies are essential.

Ultimately, international organizations and peacekeeping forces continue to strive towards a world free from wars, where conflicts are resolved through dialogue and diplomacy, laying the foundation for a more peaceful and harmonious global community.

PART 4: PREVENTING WARS AND BUILDING PEACE

CHAPTER 8: EARLY WARNING SYSTEMS

In the pursuit of a more peaceful world, early warning systems have emerged as indispensable tools for conflict prevention. This chapter delves into the significance of early warning systems, drawing on case studies to highlight successful efforts, while also acknowledging the challenges and limitations faced by these critical mechanisms.

**The Importance of Early Warning Systems in Conflict Prevention: **

Early warning systems act as proactive tools that monitor and assess potential threats to peace before they escalate into full-blown conflicts. They provide decision-makers with timely and accurate information, enabling them to take preventative measures and address underlying issues that could lead to violence.

By detecting warning signs at their nascent stages, early warning systems allow for diplomatic interventions, mediation efforts, and targeted strategies to prevent conflicts from spiralling out of control. These systems also support conflict-sensitive development, humanitarian responses, and peacebuilding initiatives.

**Case Studies of Successful Early Warning Efforts:
**

1. **United Nations Peacebuilding Commission (PBC): ** The PBC uses early warning mechanisms to identify countries at risk of relapsing into conflict. Through regular assessments and consultations, the PBC advises the UN Security Council on appropriate preventive actions and peacebuilding strategies.

2. **European Union Conflict Early Warning System (EUCS): ** The EUCS combines diplomatic reporting, open-source intelligence, and data analysis to identify potential crises in regions of interest. The EUCS has played a pivotal role in preventing conflicts in the Balkans and Africa.

3. **Crisis Group's Conflict Alert System: ** The International Crisis Group employs a unique conflict alert system that draws on its analysts' expertise and field research to identify potential crises. By issuing timely alerts, the Crisis Group helps policymakers and international actors

respond proactively to emerging conflicts.

**Challenges and Limitations of Early Warning Systems: **

While early warning systems are valuable tools, they also face challenges and limitations that must be addressed to enhance their effectiveness.

1. **Data Collection and Accuracy: ** Early warning systems rely heavily on data and information from various sources. Ensuring the accuracy and reliability of data can be challenging, especially in areas with limited access and ongoing conflict.

2. **Political Will and Response: ** Even with accurate warnings, the political will to act and respond promptly to prevent conflicts is not always guaranteed. Some decision-makers may prioritize short-term interests over conflict prevention efforts.

3. **Coordination and Communication: ** Effective early warning systems require seamless coordination and communication among various stakeholders, including governments, international organizations, and local communities. Ensuring smooth cooperation can be challenging.

4. **Conflict Complexity: ** Early warning systems may struggle to predict the dynamics of complex conflicts, involving multiple actors and deeply rooted historical grievances.

**Conclusion: **

Early warning systems play a crucial role in keeping the peace by detecting and addressing potential conflicts before they escalate. By providing timely information and analysis, these systems empower decision-makers to take preventive actions and implement targeted strategies for conflict resolution and peacebuilding.

Despite their significance, early warning systems face inherent challenges and limitations. Addressing these issues requires ongoing efforts to improve data collection, enhance coordination among stakeholders, and foster political will to respond proactively to warnings.

As technology and data analytics advance, early warning systems hold the potential to become even more effective in preventing conflicts and promoting sustainable peace. Their continued development and refinement are vital in the pursuit of a more peaceful and harmonious world, where the scourge of wars can be mitigated, if not entirely eradicated.

CHAPTER 9: CONFLICT PREVENTION STRATEGIES

In the pursuit of a more peaceful world, conflict prevention takes centre stage. This chapter explores proactive measures to prevent conflicts, the significance of addressing root causes, and the role of education and awareness in conflict prevention.

**Proactive Measures to Prevent Conflicts: **

1. **Mediation and Diplomacy: ** Early intervention through mediation and diplomatic efforts can prevent disputes from escalating into full-blown conflicts. Skilled mediators can facilitate communication and understanding between parties in conflict, seeking common ground for resolution.

2. **Dialogue and Negotiation: ** Creating

platforms for dialogue and negotiation allows conflicting parties to express their grievances, concerns, and interests. By engaging in constructive dialogue, they can work towards finding peaceful solutions.

3. **Preventive Deployment of Peacekeepers: ** The timely deployment of peacekeeping forces to potential conflict zones can deter violence and stabilize volatile situations, preventing conflicts from spiralling out of control.

**Addressing Root Causes of Conflicts: **

1. **Poverty and Inequality: ** Socio-economic disparities often fuel conflicts, especially in regions with high poverty rates and limited access to resources. Addressing poverty and promoting inclusive economic growth can significantly reduce the risk of conflicts.

2. **Social and Political Marginalization: ** Marginalized groups, such as ethnic minorities and indigenous communities, are more susceptible to conflict. Empowering marginalized communities and ensuring their representation in decision-making processes can foster social cohesion.

3. **Resource Scarcity and Competition: ** Conflicts often arise due to competition over scarce resources like water, land, and minerals. Sustainable resource management and equitable

distribution can mitigate these tensions.

**The Role of Education and Awareness in Conflict Prevention: **

1. **Promoting Tolerance and Understanding: ** Education can foster empathy, understanding, and tolerance among diverse communities. By teaching about different cultures and histories, education can combat prejudice and stereotypes.

2. **Peace Education in Schools: ** Integrating peace education into school curriculums can instil conflict resolution skills and promote a culture of peace from an early age. This empowers the youth to be future peacemakers.

3. **Media and Information Dissemination: ** Responsible and unbiased media coverage can play a critical role in preventing conflicts by disseminating accurate information and promoting peaceful narratives.

**Conclusion: **

Conflict prevention is a collective responsibility that requires proactive measures and a deep understanding of root causes. Mediation, diplomacy, and preventive deployment of peacekeepers are valuable tools to prevent conflicts before they escalate.

Addressing underlying issues such as poverty, inequality, and social marginalization is essential in breaking the cycle of violence. By empowering marginalized communities and ensuring equitable resource distribution, societies can create environments conducive to peace.

Education and awareness are powerful tools in conflict prevention. Through peace education, schools can nurture the next generation of peacemakers, equipped with conflict resolution skills and a commitment to peace.

Media also play a crucial role in shaping public opinion and perceptions. Responsible media coverage and information dissemination can promote peaceful narratives, combating misinformation and propaganda that can fuel conflicts.

In summary, conflict prevention requires a multi-faceted approach that involves all levels of society, from local communities to international organizations. By embracing proactive strategies, addressing root causes, and promoting education and awareness, we can work towards a more peaceful and harmonious world, preventing conflicts before they arise and keeping the peace for generations to come.

CHAPTER 10: BUILDING PEACEFUL COMMUNITIES

In the pursuit of sustainable peace, building peaceful communities is paramount. This chapter delves into the significance of grassroots efforts, the role of civil society organizations and NGOs, and presents case studies showcasing the transformative power of community-led peace initiatives.

**Grassroots Efforts in Building Peaceful Communities: **

1. **Local Engagement: ** Grassroots efforts involve engaging with local communities directly affected by conflicts. By actively involving community members in decision-making processes, peacebuilding initiatives become more inclusive and representative of their needs.

2. **Conflict Transformation Workshops: ** Conducting conflict transformation workshops at the community level can equip individuals with conflict resolution skills. These workshops provide a safe space for open dialogue and help bridge divides.

3. **Empowering Women and Youth: ** Empowering women and youth in peacebuilding efforts is crucial. Women play a significant role in conflict prevention, resolution, and peacekeeping.

**The Role of Civil Society Organizations and NGOs: **

1. **Advocacy and Awareness: ** Civil society organizations and NGOs advocate for peace and amplify the voices of those affected by conflicts. They raise awareness about the consequences of war and mobilize support for peaceful solutions.

2. **Resource Mobilization: ** NGOs play a vital role in mobilizing resources for peacebuilding initiatives. They seek funding for projects that address the root causes of conflicts and promote reconciliation.

3. **Neutral Mediators: ** Civil society organizations often act as neutral mediators between conflicting parties, facilitating dialogue and negotiation.

**Case Studies of Community-Led Peace Initiatives:

**

1. **The Peace Community of San José de Apartadó, Colombia:** During Colombia's decades-long armed conflict, the Peace Community of San José de Apartadó established a self-declared neutral zone. This community-led initiative aims to protect civilians from violence and advocates for peace.

2. **The Ubuntu Women Shelter, Kenya: ** The Ubuntu Women Shelter in Kenya provides refuge and support to women fleeing violence and conflict. By empowering women with education and vocational training, the shelter promotes self-reliance and community integration.

3. **Seeds of Peace, Middle East: ** Seeds of Peace is a program that brings together young leaders from conflict-affected regions, such as Israel and Palestine. Through dialogue and experiential learning, the program fosters understanding and cooperation among future change-makers.

**Conclusion: **

Building peaceful communities is the foundation of sustainable peace on a broader scale. Grassroots efforts that engage local communities directly, empower women and youth, and address the root causes of conflicts are vital in creating environments where peace can flourish.

Civil society organizations and NGOs play a pivotal

role in advocating for peace, mobilizing resources, and acting as neutral mediators. Their work complements the efforts of governments and international organizations, enhancing the overall effectiveness of peacebuilding initiatives.

Case studies of community-led peace initiatives demonstrate that change begins at the local level. From conflict-ridden regions in Colombia to war-torn areas in the Middle East, ordinary individuals and grassroots organizations have proven that peace is achievable even in the most challenging circumstances.

By promoting community-led peace initiatives, societies can foster a sense of ownership over the peacebuilding process. As we recognize the power of communities to transform conflicts, we become better equipped to build a more peaceful and harmonious world.

PART 5: POST-CONFLICT RECONSTRUCTION

CHAPTER 11: TRANSITIONAL JUSTICE

In the aftermath of conflicts, societies must come to terms with the atrocities committed and the widespread human rights violations that occurred. Transitional justice provides a framework for addressing these issues, promoting healing, and moving towards a more peaceful future. This chapter delves into the concept of transitional justice, truth, and reconciliation commissions, and the importance of accountability for war crimes and human rights violations.

**The Concept of Transitional Justice: **

Transitional justice refers to the set of measures and processes used to address past human rights abuses and promote reconciliation in societies transitioning from conflict to peace. It acknowledges the need to confront the legacy of violence, uphold human rights, and foster social cohesion.

**Truth and Reconciliation Commissions: **

Truth and Reconciliation Commissions (TRCs) are an essential component of transitional justice. These independent bodies are tasked with investigating and documenting human rights violations, abuses, and other crimes committed during the conflict. TRCs provide victims and perpetrators with the opportunity to testify and share their experiences.

The process of truth-telling and acknowledgment of past wrongs aims to promote healing and foster a shared understanding of the conflict's causes and consequences. By revealing the truth, TRCs can help break the cycle of violence and contribute to national reconciliation.

**Accountability for War Crimes and Human Rights Violations: **

Promoting accountability for war crimes and human rights violations is crucial for preventing future conflicts and upholding justice. Perpetrators of egregious crimes must face legal consequences for their actions. This includes prosecuting those responsible for genocide, war crimes, crimes against humanity, and other serious offenses.

International courts, such as the International

Criminal Court (ICC), play a vital role in prosecuting individuals accused of international crimes. National courts also have a responsibility to hold perpetrators accountable and provide justice to victims.

Ensuring accountability also involves reparations for victims, including compensation, rehabilitation, and support to rebuild their lives. This helps victims regain their dignity and rebuild trust in society.

**Challenges and Limitations: **

Transitional justice faces several challenges and limitations. One significant challenge is striking a balance between justice and peace. In some cases, pursuing accountability may impede peace negotiations, making it challenging to find a delicate equilibrium.

Another challenge lies in securing the cooperation of state authorities and international support for transitional justice initiatives. Political resistance and lack of resources can hinder the effectiveness of truth commissions and accountability efforts.

Additionally, transitional justice processes must be inclusive and address the needs and rights of all affected communities, including marginalized groups and minorities. Failure to include all stakeholders can lead to further grievances and tensions.

**Conclusion: **

Transitional justice is a vital mechanism for addressing the legacy of violence and human rights abuses in societies emerging from conflicts. Truth and reconciliation commissions play a central role in providing a platform for truth-telling and fostering reconciliation. Accountability for war crimes and human rights violations is crucial for preventing impunity and ensuring justice for victims.

Despite the challenges and limitations, transitional justice remains an essential tool in building sustainable peace and promoting respect for human rights. By confronting the past, societies can pave the way for a more just, inclusive, and peaceful future. Transitional justice is not just about stopping wars; it is about building a foundation for lasting peace and preventing conflicts from resurfacing in the years to come.

CHAPTER 12: REBUILDING SOCIETIES AFTER WAR

The aftermath of war leaves societies devastated, with shattered infrastructure, fractured institutions, and broken trust. Rebuilding these societies is a monumental task that requires careful planning, cooperation, and perseverance. This chapter explores the challenges of post-conflict reconstruction, the process of rebuilding infrastructure and institutions, and the crucial role of international aid and support in these efforts.

**Challenges of Post-Conflict Reconstruction: **

Post-conflict reconstruction is fraught with numerous challenges that make the task complex and daunting. One significant challenge is the sheer scale of destruction left behind by war.

Homes, schools, hospitals, and essential services are often reduced to rubble, leaving communities struggling to meet their basic needs.

Additionally, the economy may be in shambles, and the loss of livelihoods can lead to poverty and desperation. Addressing the root causes of the conflict, such as political grievances and social inequalities, is essential to creating a stable and inclusive society.

Another challenge lies in managing expectations. After years of conflict and suffering, people want to see immediate change and progress. However, reconstruction is a slow and arduous process that requires time and patience.

**Rebuilding Infrastructure, Institutions, and Trust: **

Rebuilding infrastructure is a critical aspect of post-conflict reconstruction. Roads, bridges, schools, and hospitals must be reconstructed to restore essential services and facilitate economic development. This requires significant investment and coordination between various actors.

Institutions, including the judiciary, police force, and public administration, may have been deeply affected by the conflict. Restoring and strengthening these institutions is crucial for establishing the rule of law and ensuring good governance.

Equally important is rebuilding trust among communities that were divided by the conflict. Reconciliation efforts, truth and reconciliation commissions, and community dialogues can play a significant role in healing wounds and fostering a sense of unity and solidarity.

**The Role of International Aid and Support: **

International aid and support are instrumental in post-conflict reconstruction. In many cases, war-torn countries lack the resources and expertise to undertake reconstruction efforts on their own. International organizations, donor countries, and non-governmental organizations (NGOs) play a crucial role in providing financial assistance, technical expertise, and humanitarian aid.

However, international aid also poses challenges. Coordinating multiple aid efforts can be complex, and there is a risk of aid dependency if countries become reliant on external assistance. Ensuring that aid is used effectively and transparently is vital to maximizing its impact.

International support can also extend to peacekeeping missions that help maintain stability and security during the early stages of post-conflict reconstruction. Peacekeepers play a vital role in protecting civilians, monitoring ceasefires, and facilitating the delivery of humanitarian aid.

**Conclusion: **

Rebuilding societies after war is a formidable task that requires dedication, cooperation, and long-term commitment. Addressing the challenges of post-conflict reconstruction, rebuilding infrastructure and institutions, and fostering trust and unity among communities are essential steps towards sustainable peace.

International aid and support are indispensable in these efforts, but they must be provided responsibly and in coordination with the affected country's priorities and needs. Ultimately, the success of post-conflict reconstruction depends on the collective efforts of governments, civil society, international organizations, and the global community in working towards a common goal of lasting peace and stability.

PART 6: THE ROLE OF EDUCATION AND MEDIA

CHAPTER 13: PEACE EDUCATION

In a world plagued by conflicts and violence, peace education emerges as a powerful tool to sow the seeds of tolerance, empathy, and non-violence in the hearts and minds of young generations. This chapter delves into the significance of peace education in schools and universities, the teaching of conflict resolution skills, and the profound impact such education can have on society.

**The Importance of Peace Education in Schools and Universities: **

Peace education is an essential component of a comprehensive curriculum that seeks to shape well-rounded individuals capable of critical thinking and empathy. By integrating peace education into the educational system, schools and universities can foster a culture of peace and understanding.

One of the primary objectives of peace education is to raise awareness about the destructive consequences of conflicts and violence. Through age-appropriate discussions and activities, students can gain a deeper understanding of the complexities of war and its impact on individuals and communities.

Moreover, peace education encourages open dialogue about historical and contemporary conflicts, promoting a more inclusive and tolerant society. By studying conflicts from multiple perspectives, students learn to challenge biases and stereotypes, fostering mutual respect among diverse groups.

**Teaching Conflict Resolution Skills to Young Generations: **

Conflict resolution skills are at the core of peace education. By imparting these skills to young generations, educators empower them to address disagreements and differences constructively. Conflict resolution education equips students with negotiation, mediation, and communication skills, enabling them to resolve disputes without resorting to violence.

Practicing conflict resolution in a controlled environment helps students develop emotional intelligence and self-awareness. They learn to manage their emotions effectively and approach conflicts with a calm and rational mindset.

Peace education also emphasizes the importance of active listening and empathy. By learning to put themselves in others' shoes, students gain a deeper understanding of their peers' perspectives, strengthening social bonds and reducing hostility.

**The Impact of Peace Education on Society: **

The benefits of peace education extend far beyond the classroom, leaving a lasting impact on society. As students grow into responsible citizens, their understanding of peace and conflict resolution influences their interactions with others and their engagement in societal issues.

In communities where peace education is embraced, there is a noticeable decrease in violence and a greater emphasis on cooperation and collaboration. Students who have undergone peace education are more likely to reject violence as a means of resolving disputes and are better equipped to engage in constructive dialogues.

Peace education also fosters a sense of social responsibility, inspiring students to become advocates for peace and agents of positive change. They may engage in community service projects, participate in peacebuilding initiatives, and take an active role in promoting tolerance and diversity.

**Conclusion: **

Peace education holds the key to building a more peaceful and harmonious world. By integrating peace education into the educational system, we can raise a generation of individuals who understand the true cost of wars and violence and who possess the skills and empathy needed to resolve conflicts peacefully.

Investing in peace education is an investment in the future of our societies. By empowering young generations with conflict resolution skills and promoting a culture of peace, we pave the way for a more inclusive, tolerant, and compassionate world where differences are celebrated, and violence is replaced with understanding. As educators, policymakers, and global citizens, we must unite in our commitment to peace education and work together to keep the flame of hope for a peaceful future burning brightly.

CHAPTER 14: MEDIA AND PEACE JOURNALISM

In the digital age, media plays a pivotal role in shaping public opinion and influencing conflicts around the world. This chapter explores the complex relationship between media and conflicts, the impact of media coverage on shaping narratives, and the concept of peace journalism as a potential tool in promoting peace.

**The Role of Media in Conflict Reporting: **

Media has the power to inform, educate, and mobilize people on a global scale. In conflict zones, journalists often become the primary source of information for the rest of the world. Their reports provide critical insights into the realities faced by communities affected by conflicts.

However, media's role in conflict reporting

is not without challenges. Journalists must navigate ethical dilemmas, safety risks, and issues of impartiality while covering conflicts. Sensationalism and biased reporting can exacerbate tensions and perpetuate stereotypes, making it crucial for media professionals to approach their work with responsibility and integrity.

**The Impact of Media Coverage on Conflicts: **

Media coverage can significantly influence the course and perception of conflicts. Sensationalized reporting can intensify fear and anger among audiences, contributing to the escalation of violence. Conversely, unbiased, and balanced reporting can shed light on the root causes of conflicts and promote understanding.

The ubiquity of social media has further amplified the impact of media on conflicts. Misinformation and fake news can spread rapidly, fuelling hatred and division. On the other hand, social media platforms have become powerful tools for activists and peacebuilders to share stories of hope, unity, and reconciliation.

**The Concept of Peace Journalism: **

Peace journalism presents an alternative approach to reporting conflicts. It emphasizes constructive and solutions-oriented reporting, seeking to promote understanding and dialogue rather than fuelling hatred and animosity.

Peace journalism aims to give voice to all parties involved in conflicts, providing a platform for marginalized voices and perspectives. It seeks to humanize the "enemy" and highlight the common ground between conflicting parties. By focusing on peacebuilding efforts and positive stories of resilience and reconciliation, peace journalism offers a more nuanced and balanced view of conflicts.

**The Potential of Peace Journalism in Promoting Peace: **

Peace journalism has the potential to be a powerful tool in promoting peace and conflict resolution. By reframing narratives and challenging stereotypes, peace journalism can bridge divides and build empathy among diverse audiences.

Moreover, peace journalism can empower communities affected by conflicts to share their experiences and aspirations for peace. By amplifying local voices, media can foster a sense of agency and ownership in peacebuilding efforts.

To fully realize the potential of peace journalism, media organizations and journalists must adopt a conscious and ethical approach to reporting conflicts. This includes rigorous fact-checking, sensitivity to cultural nuances, and avoiding sensationalism.

**Conclusion: **

Media wields immense power in shaping public perceptions and attitudes towards conflicts. The impact of media coverage on conflicts can either exacerbate tensions or promote understanding and reconciliation.

Peace journalism offers an alternative approach that seeks to bridge divides and promote peace through constructive and unbiased reporting. By humanizing the experiences of those affected by conflicts and highlighting peacebuilding efforts, media can play a vital role in creating a more peaceful and harmonious world.

As consumers of media, we must remain critical and discerning, seeking out reliable and balanced sources of information. By supporting ethical and responsible journalism, we can contribute to the promotion of peace and understanding in our interconnected world.

PART 7: CASE STUDIES OF SUCCESSFUL PEACEKEEPING AND CONFLICT RESOLUTION

CHAPTER 15: THE PEACE PROCESS IN NORTHERN IRELAND

The Northern Ireland conflict, also known as the Troubles, was a protracted and deeply entrenched conflict that spanned several decades. The chapter delves into the historical context of the conflict, the arduous journey towards peace, and the valuable lessons learned from the Northern Ireland peace process.

**The Historical Context of the Northern Ireland Conflict: **

The Northern Ireland conflict had its roots in centuries-old divisions between the Protestant unionists, who sought to remain part of the United Kingdom, and the Catholic nationalists, who sought a united Ireland. The struggle for political and religious identity escalated into violence and deep-seated animosities.

From the late 1960s to the late 1990s, Northern Ireland was ravaged by bombings, shootings, and sectarian violence. The conflict left thousands of dead, many more injured, and entire communities torn apart.

**The Peace Process and the Good Friday Agreement: **

Amidst the turmoil, a ray of hope emerged with the initiation of the peace process. The peace talks aimed to find a resolution that could bring an end to the violence and pave the way for lasting peace and reconciliation.

The Good Friday Agreement, signed on April 10, 1998, marked a historic milestone in the peace process. It provided a framework for power-sharing between unionists and nationalists, established new institutions, and addressed contentious issues such as policing and human rights.

The agreement also set in motion a series of decommissioning processes to disarm paramilitary groups and establish a more stable and inclusive political landscape.

**Lessons Learned from the Northern Ireland Peace Process: **

The Northern Ireland peace process offers

invaluable lessons in conflict resolution and peacebuilding:

1. **Inclusivity and Dialogue: ** The success of the peace process was built on inclusive dialogue that involved all parties, including political leaders, community representatives, and civil society organizations. By engaging diverse stakeholders, the negotiations achieved a more comprehensive and sustainable peace.

2. **Building Trust: ** Trust-building was central to the peace process. It required difficult compromises and a willingness to listen and understand each other's grievances. The establishment of cross-community relationships laid the groundwork for a shared vision of peace.

3. **Third-Party Mediation: ** The involvement of neutral third-party mediators, including the United States and the Irish and British governments, played a crucial role in facilitating negotiations and bridging divides.

4. **Addressing Root Causes: ** The Good Friday Agreement tackled the root causes of the conflict, addressing issues of identity, political representation, and socio-economic disparities. By confronting these underlying issues, the peace process aimed to create a more just and equitable society.

5. **Consolidating Peace: ** The peace process

did not end with the signing of the Good Friday Agreement. It required ongoing efforts to implement the agreement's provisions, build institutions, and foster reconciliation. The commitment to peace was a long-term endeavour.

**Conclusion: **

The Northern Ireland peace process stands as a testament to the power of dialogue, compromise, and reconciliation in resolving seemingly intractable conflicts. It showcases the importance of inclusivity, trust-building, and third-party mediation in reaching peaceful resolutions.

While the journey towards peace was challenging and required immense effort, the peace process in Northern Ireland demonstrates that sustainable peace is possible when there is a shared commitment to building a more harmonious and inclusive society.

The lessons learned from the Northern Ireland peace process continue to resonate worldwide, inspiring peacebuilders and negotiators to pursue peaceful solutions in even the most entrenched conflicts. By drawing on these lessons, we can work towards a more peaceful world where wars are replaced by dialogue, understanding, and cooperation.

CHAPTER 16: THE DIPLOMATIC RESOLUTION OF THE CUBAN MISSILE CRISIS

**Overview of the Cuban Missile Crisis: **

The Cuban Missile Crisis, which occurred in October 1962, was a pivotal moment during the Cold War when the world stood on the brink of nuclear war. The crisis was triggered when the United States discovered that the Soviet Union had placed nuclear missiles in Cuba, just 90 miles off the coast of Florida. This development posed a grave threat to U.S. national security, and tensions escalated rapidly between the two superpowers.

**The Role of Diplomacy in Resolving the Crisis: **

Amidst the heightened tensions, both the United

States and the Soviet Union recognized the catastrophic consequences of a nuclear conflict. Diplomacy played a crucial role in finding a peaceful resolution to the crisis. President John F. Kennedy and Soviet Premier Nikita Khrushchev engaged in a series of back-channel communications to de-escalate the situation and seek a path towards peace.

Rather than resorting to immediate military action, both leaders understood the significance of exploring diplomatic options. They recognized that open dialogue and negotiation were vital in finding a resolution that would avoid a global catastrophe.

**The Importance of Communication and Negotiation in Avoiding War: **

The Cuban Missile Crisis stands as a testament to the critical importance of communication and negotiation in avoiding war. Instead of acting impulsively and reacting to provocations, Kennedy and Khrushchev maintained open channels of communication. They exchanged letters and utilized intermediaries to prevent misunderstandings and miscalculations.

Through these diplomatic exchanges, both leaders were able to convey their concerns and intentions clearly, which helped dispel misconceptions and misperceptions. This open communication was pivotal in preventing further escalation and laying the groundwork for a potential resolution.

**The Back-Channel Negotiations: **

One of the most critical aspects of the diplomatic resolution was the use of back-channel negotiations. To avoid public posturing and save face, Kennedy and Khrushchev utilized secret channels of communication. The two leaders exchanged letters and messages through intermediaries, allowing them to discuss potential solutions without the pressure of public scrutiny.

These back-channel negotiations provided a safe space for both sides to explore possible concessions and compromises. It allowed them to find common ground and avoid becoming entrenched in positions that could have led to a disastrous confrontation.

**The Compromise: **

Through the diplomatic efforts and back-channel negotiations, a resolution was reached. The Soviet Union agreed to remove its nuclear missiles from Cuba, and in return, the United States promised not to invade Cuba and agreed to remove its own nuclear missiles from Turkey.

This compromise was a diplomatic triumph, as it allowed both superpowers to save face and de-escalate the crisis without resorting to military conflict. It also set a precedent for future negotiations during the Cold War, demonstrating that diplomatic solutions were possible even in the most perilous situations.

**Conclusion: **

The diplomatic resolution of the Cuban Missile Crisis stands as a shining example of how communication and negotiation can avert catastrophic conflicts. By keeping the lines of communication open, Kennedy and Khrushchev were able to find common ground and defuse tensions.

The crisis serves as a reminder that diplomacy is an essential tool in resolving conflicts and avoiding war. It underscores the importance of seeking peaceful resolutions through dialogue, compromise, and understanding. The lessons from the Cuban Missile Crisis continue to resonate today, offering valuable insights into the power of diplomacy in keeping the peace and preventing war.

PART 8: THE ROLE OF WOMEN IN PEACEBUILDING

CHAPTER 17: WOMEN AS PEACEBUILDERS

In the quest for sustainable peace, the role of women as peacebuilders cannot be underestimated. Throughout history, women have played significant but often overlooked roles in conflict prevention, resolution, and peacekeeping efforts. This chapter explores the invaluable contributions of women to the peacebuilding process and highlights the importance of gender equality in creating lasting and sustainable peace.

**The Role of Women in Conflict Prevention and Resolution: **

Women have been at the forefront of conflict prevention, utilizing their unique perspectives and experiences to identify early warning signs and address underlying causes of violence. Women's organizations and grassroots movements have been instrumental in advocating for peace, often working tirelessly to bridge divides and foster understanding among conflicting parties.

Research has shown that peace processes are more successful and sustainable when women are involved. Women's participation brings diverse viewpoints and a focus on building inclusive solutions that prioritize the needs of all members of society. Their ability to build relationships and promote dialogue makes them natural mediators and peacemakers.

**Women's Contributions to Peace Negotiations and Peacekeeping: **

Despite facing challenges and barriers, women have made significant strides in peace negotiations and peacekeeping operations. Women negotiators have been successful in facilitating dialogue between conflicting parties and shaping peace agreements that address the needs of vulnerable groups, including women and children.

In peacekeeping missions, women have proven to be effective in building trust within communities and gaining access to critical information. Female peacekeepers serve as role models, inspiring women, and girls in conflict-affected areas to envision a future beyond violence and instability.

**The Importance of Gender Equality in Building

Sustainable Peace: **

Gender equality is not only a human right but also a crucial component of sustainable peace. In societies where women are marginalized or excluded from decision-making processes, conflicts tend to be more prolonged and devastating. Conversely, societies that prioritize gender equality are more likely to achieve lasting peace and development.

Empowering women economically and politically strengthens societies. When women are given equal opportunities and representation, they can contribute their unique perspectives, knowledge, and skills to rebuilding communities torn apart by conflict.

**Overcoming Challenges and Advancing Women's Role in Peacebuilding: **

Despite the progress made, women still face challenges in their efforts to promote peace. They may encounter discrimination, limited access to resources, and cultural barriers that hinder their full participation in peacebuilding processes. It is essential to address these challenges and create an enabling environment that empowers women to become effective agents of peace.

Governments, international organizations, and civil society must work together to promote gender-responsive policies and initiatives that advance women's participation in conflict prevention and resolution. Investing in education and training for women in conflict-affected areas can equip them with the skills and confidence to contribute meaningfully to peacebuilding efforts.

**Conclusion: **

In the journey towards a more peaceful world, women's role as peacebuilders is indispensable. Their contributions in conflict prevention, peace negotiations, and peacekeeping have demonstrated that sustainable peace can only be achieved through inclusive and gender-responsive approaches.

As we strive to stop wars and keep the peace, we must recognize and celebrate the invaluable contributions of women. By embracing gender equality and empowering women as leaders and agents of change, we can build a future where peace and prosperity thrive for all. Women's voices and experiences must be valued and integrated into all aspects of peacebuilding, laying the foundation for a more peaceful and just world.

CHAPTER 18: WOMEN, PEACE, AND SECURITY AGENDA

The Women, Peace, and Security (WPS) Agenda, spearheaded by the United Nations Security Council Resolution 1325, represents a pivotal milestone in recognizing and addressing the unique experiences of women in conflict and their vital role in building sustainable peace. This chapter delves into the significance of the WPS Agenda, its implementation, and the challenges and progress in advancing the role of women in peacebuilding.

**Overview of UN Security Council Resolution 1325: **

Adopted unanimously in October 2000, UN Security Council Resolution 1325 was a groundbreaking moment for the recognition of women's contributions to peace and security. The resolution reaffirms the importance of women's equal participation and full involvement in all efforts to maintain and promote peace and security.

Key provisions of Resolution 1325 include the protection of women and girls during conflict, prevention of violence against women, increased participation of women in peace negotiations and peacekeeping operations, and the consideration of gender perspectives in peace processes.

**The Implementation of the Women, Peace, and Security Agenda: **

Since its adoption, the WPS Agenda has seen both progress and challenges in its implementation. Many countries have developed National Action Plans (NAPs) to guide their efforts in promoting women's participation in peacebuilding and conflict resolution.

Efforts have been made to increase the number of women in peacekeeping missions and leadership roles. Female peacekeepers have proven to be effective in engaging with local communities and addressing the unique needs of women and children affected by conflict.

Additionally, women-led civil society organizations have played a critical role in advocating for peace and promoting gender equality. Their contributions to conflict prevention, mediation, and peacebuilding efforts have been invaluable.

**Challenges and Progress in Advancing the Role of Women in Peacebuilding: **

While progress has been made, significant challenges persist in advancing the role of women in peacebuilding. Women continue to face barriers to their meaningful participation in peace processes, including discrimination, exclusion from decision-making, and limited access to resources.

The representation of women in peace negotiations remains low, with only a small percentage of negotiators and mediators being women. This lack of representation hinders the inclusion of women's perspectives and concerns in peace agreements.

Moreover, women are often disproportionately affected by conflict-related sexual violence, which underscores the need for greater efforts in protecting and supporting survivors.

However, there have been inspiring examples of women's leadership and agency in peacebuilding. From Liberia to Colombia, women have been at the forefront of peace movements, advocating for reconciliation and social transformation. Their initiatives have had a lasting impact on post-conflict societies, fostering healing and resilience.

**Conclusion: **

The Women, Peace, and Security Agenda serves as a powerful tool in promoting gender equality, preventing conflict, and building sustainable peace. However, to fully realize its potential, it is crucial to address the challenges that hinder women's meaningful participation in peacebuilding processes.

Investing in women's education, leadership, and economic empowerment is essential for creating an environment where women can actively contribute to peacebuilding efforts. Increasing the representation of women in decision-making positions and peace negotiations is vital to ensure that women's voices are heard, and their concerns addressed.

As we continue our journey towards stopping wars and keeping the peace, the empowerment and inclusion of women must remain a central pillar of our efforts. By recognizing and supporting the vital role of women in peacebuilding, we can forge a path towards a more just, equal, and peaceful world for all.

PART 9: DISARMAMENT AND ARMS CONTROL

CHAPTER 19: DISARMAMENT EFFORTS

In the pursuit of peace and security, disarmament plays a pivotal role in preventing wars and mitigating the devastating impact of conflicts. This chapter delves into the importance of disarmament, the role of arms control agreements and treaties, and the challenges in achieving global disarmament.

**The Importance of Disarmament in Preventing Wars: **

Disarmament refers to the reduction or elimination of military weapons and equipment, ranging from small arms to nuclear weapons. Its primary objective is to reduce the potential for armed conflicts and create an environment conducive to peaceful resolution of disputes.

The presence of a vast array of weapons in a region or globally can exacerbate tensions and trigger a sense of insecurity among nations. By reducing the stockpiles of weaponry, disarmament diminishes the likelihood of conflicts arising from misunderstandings, miscalculations, or arms races.

Moreover, the diversion of resources towards arms production and maintenance often comes at the expense of social and economic development. By diverting these resources to peaceful endeavours, disarmament can contribute to sustainable development and the well-being of societies.

**The Role of Arms Control Agreements and Treaties: **

Arms control agreements and treaties are instrumental in achieving disarmament goals. These agreements establish legally binding commitments between nations to limit the production, transfer, and deployment of specific types of weapons.

One of the most notable arms control agreements is the Treaty on the Non-Proliferation of nuclear weapons (NPT), which aims to prevent the spread of nuclear weapons and promote disarmament. Another significant treaty is the Arms Trade Treaty (ATT), designed to regulate the international trade in conventional weapons and prevent their illicit transfer to unauthorized entities.

Additionally, regional arms control arrangements, such as the Treaty on Conventional Armed Forces in Europe (CFE), have contributed to stability and confidence-building measures in specific regions.

**The Challenges in Achieving Global Disarmament: **

While disarmament efforts are crucial for peacebuilding, they face several challenges that hinder progress towards global disarmament.

Firstly, vested interests in the arms industry and national security considerations often complicate disarmament negotiations. Countries with significant arms industries may resist disarmament measures due to the economic and political implications of reducing military spending.

Secondly, mistrust and geopolitical rivalries among nations can undermine disarmament efforts. States may be reluctant to disarm if they perceive security threats from other nations and believe that maintaining strong military capabilities is necessary for their defence.

Thirdly, the lack of transparency in arms transfers and the proliferation of illicit arms networks pose challenges to arms control efforts. Identifying and curbing the flow of weapons to non-state actors and unauthorized entities requires international cooperation and intelligence-sharing.

**Conclusion: **

Disarmament efforts are an integral part of keeping the peace and preventing wars. By reducing the availability of weapons and fostering an environment of trust and cooperation, disarmament initiatives contribute to international security and stability.

Arms control agreements and treaties play a crucial role in achieving disarmament goals and establishing norms for responsible arms behaviour. However, global disarmament remains an ambitious and complex task that demands sustained commitment and collaboration from the international community.

To overcome the challenges hindering disarmament progress, diplomatic dialogue, confidence-building measures, and increased transparency are essential. Ultimately, a world free from the threat of war and violence is possible through collective efforts to prioritize peace, security, and disarmament.

CHAPTER 20: NUCLEAR NON-PROLIFERATION AND PEACE

In an ever-evolving geopolitical landscape, the spectre of nuclear weapons casts a long shadow over global security and peace. Chapter 20 explores the impact of nuclear weapons on international stability, the efforts to prevent nuclear proliferation, and the pivotal role of diplomacy and international cooperation in nuclear disarmament.

**The Impact of nuclear weapons on Global Security: **

The development and use of nuclear weapons during World War II demonstrated the catastrophic consequences of these powerful and indiscriminate devices. Since then, the world has grappled with the implications of nuclear warfare and the potential for unprecedented destruction.

The possession of nuclear weapons by nations has altered the dynamics of international relations, leading to the establishment of a nuclear deterrence doctrine. The idea of mutually assured destruction (MAD) posits that the possession of nuclear capabilities deters adversaries from launching an attack due to the certainty of overwhelming retaliation.

However, the existence of nuclear weapons also generates a heightened sense of insecurity and fear among nations. The possibility of nuclear proliferation to unstable or hostile states raises concerns about accidental or deliberate use, leading to regional or global instability.

**The Efforts to Prevent Nuclear Proliferation: **

The international community has undertaken various initiatives to prevent the spread of nuclear weapons and promote nuclear disarmament. The Treaty on the Non-Proliferation of nuclear weapons (NPT) stands as a cornerstone of these efforts. The NPT aims to prevent the proliferation of nuclear weapons to non-nuclear-weapon states while fostering disarmament commitments among nuclear-weapon states.

Additionally, nuclear-weapon-free zones (NWFZs) have been established in different regions to prohibit the deployment and testing of nuclear weapons within designated areas. These zones enhance regional security by creating confidence-building measures and promoting peaceful coexistence.

Efforts to prevent nuclear proliferation extend to curbing the spread of nuclear technology and knowledge. The International Atomic Energy Agency (IAEA) plays a critical role in monitoring and verifying nuclear programs to ensure they are used for peaceful purposes only.

**The Role of Diplomacy and International Cooperation in Nuclear Disarmament: **

Diplomacy and international cooperation are paramount in achieving meaningful progress in nuclear disarmament. Bilateral and multilateral negotiations have led to several landmark disarmament agreements, such as the Strategic Arms Reduction Treaty (START) and the New START between the United States and Russia.

Through diplomatic dialogue, nations can build trust, transparency, and confidence in their disarmament commitments. Verification mechanisms and arms control inspections help ensure compliance with disarmament agreements.

International cooperation is essential in addressing proliferation challenges. The Iran nuclear deal, formally known as the

Joint Comprehensive Plan of Action (JCPOA), exemplifies the importance of collective efforts to prevent the acquisition of nuclear weapons by a specific state.

**Conclusion: **

The pursuit of nuclear non-proliferation and disarmament is an urgent imperative for safeguarding global security and maintaining peace. The impact of nuclear weapons on international relations cannot be overstated, and concerted efforts are required to prevent their further proliferation.

By adhering to treaties such as the NPT, strengthening nuclear safeguards, and engaging in diplomatic dialogue, nations can lay the groundwork for a world free from the threat of nuclear conflict. The shared responsibility to prevent nuclear proliferation and promote disarmament underscores the need for sustained international cooperation and commitment to building a safer and more peaceful world.

PART 10: PEACEBUILDING AND CONFLICT RESOLUTION IN THE DIGITAL AGE

CHAPTER 21: TECHNOLOGY AND CONFLICT RESOLUTION

In the digital age, technology has become an influential tool in shaping the landscape of conflict resolution and peacebuilding. This chapter delves into the potential of technology in facilitating conflict resolution, the role of social media in peacebuilding efforts, and the challenges and ethical considerations that arise when using technology to promote peace.

**The Potential of Technology in Facilitating Conflict Resolution: **

Advancements in technology have revolutionized the way conflicts are addressed and resolved. Digital platforms offer innovative methods for communication, collaboration, and information dissemination, making them valuable assets in conflict resolution efforts.

One significant advantage of technology is its ability to connect individuals and groups across geographic boundaries. Video conferencing and virtual meetings enable diplomats, mediators, and stakeholders to engage in dialogue without the need for physical proximity, fostering more inclusive and efficient negotiations.

Moreover, technology facilitates data collection and analysis, providing valuable insights into conflict dynamics, root causes, and potential solutions. Data-driven approaches empower policymakers and peacebuilders to make informed decisions based on evidence and trends, enhancing the effectiveness of conflict resolution initiatives.

The Role of social media in Peacebuilding Efforts:

Social media platforms have emerged as powerful tools for peacebuilding and promoting dialogue among diverse communities. Through social media, individuals can share their experiences, concerns, and aspirations, creating spaces for mutual understanding and empathy.

During times of conflict, social media can serve as a platform for peace advocacy and awareness. Hashtags and online campaigns enable activists to raise awareness about ongoing conflicts and mobilize support for peaceful resolutions.

Additionally, social media can amplify the voices of marginalized communities and provide a platform for dialogue between conflicting parties. Digital spaces facilitate cross-cultural interactions, promoting tolerance and empathy among individuals from different backgrounds.

**Challenges and Ethical Considerations in Using Technology for Peacebuilding: **

While technology offers tremendous potential for conflict resolution, it also presents several challenges and ethical considerations that must be carefully navigated.

One of the primary challenges is ensuring equal access to technology across all communities. The digital divide, where certain populations lack access to technology and the internet, can exacerbate existing inequalities and hinder inclusive peacebuilding efforts.

Moreover, the rapid dissemination of information through social media can lead to misinformation and polarization. Peacebuilders must be vigilant in verifying information and countering the spread of rumours that may fuel tensions.

Ethical considerations also arise concerning data privacy and security. Confidential peace negotiations and sensitive information must be protected from cyber threats and malicious actors who may seek to disrupt peacebuilding efforts.

**Conclusion: **

The integration of technology into conflict resolution and peacebuilding initiatives offers immense promise for fostering sustainable peace. Digital platforms enable more inclusive and accessible dialogues, bridging gaps between conflicting parties and amplifying the voices of those affected by conflicts.

However, peacebuilders must navigate challenges related to access, misinformation, and data security to harness technology's potential effectively. Ethical considerations must be at the forefront of technology-driven peacebuilding efforts to ensure that information is used responsibly and that all communities can participate in shaping peaceful solutions.

As technology continues to evolve, its role in conflict resolution will become increasingly significant. Embracing technology as a complementary tool alongside traditional diplomatic methods can lead to more holistic and innovative approaches to building and sustaining peace in our interconnected world. By leveraging technology's power, we can advance the vision of a harmonious and conflict-free global community.

CHAPTER 22: CYBERSECURITY AND PEACE

In the rapidly evolving landscape of global security, the emergence of cyber warfare has become a significant concern for maintaining peace. This chapter explores the impact of cyber warfare on international security, the role of cybersecurity in preventing cyber conflicts and attacks, and the importance of international cooperation in addressing cyber threats for maintaining peace.

**The Emergence of Cyber Warfare and its Impact on Global Security: **

Cyber warfare, a form of conflict conducted in the digital domain, has grown increasingly prevalent in recent years. State and non-state actors alike are leveraging the power of cyberspace to target critical infrastructure, disrupt communications, and steal sensitive information.

The unique nature of cyber warfare allows perpetrators to operate from behind anonymous screens, making attribution challenging. This anonymity has emboldened malicious actors to launch attacks with relative impunity, posing a severe challenge to global security and peace.

**The Role of Cybersecurity in Preventing Cyber Conflicts and Attacks: **

As cyber threats continue to escalate, the importance of robust cybersecurity measures cannot be overstated. Effective cybersecurity practices are essential in preventing cyber conflicts and attacks that have the potential to escalate into larger geopolitical disputes.

Implementing strong cybersecurity protocols is critical for safeguarding critical infrastructure, government systems, and private networks. Cybersecurity measures such as encryption, firewalls, and intrusion detection systems play a crucial role in thwarting cyber-attacks and ensuring the integrity of digital systems.

Moreover, cybersecurity awareness and education are vital for individuals and organizations to recognize and respond to potential cyber threats proactively. Building a cyber-resilient society involves training citizens to identify phishing attempts, social engineering, and other common cyber-attack methods.

**The Importance of International Cooperation in Addressing Cyber Threats: **

In an interconnected world, cyber threats transcend national borders, necessitating international cooperation in addressing cyber warfare and its implications for peace. The global nature of cyberspace means that no country can effectively tackle cyber threats in isolation.

International collaboration is essential for sharing information on emerging cyber threats, coordinating incident response efforts, and developing best practices for cybersecurity. Forums such as the United Nations and other international organizations play a crucial role in fostering dialogue and collaboration among nations to address cyber threats collectively.

Furthermore, the establishment of cyber norms and rules of engagement is critical for preventing misunderstandings and unintended escalations in the cyber domain. Countries must work together to develop frameworks that govern responsible state behaviour in cyberspace and establish consequences for malicious cyber activities.

**Conclusion: **

Cybersecurity has emerged as a cornerstone for maintaining peace in the digital age. The rise of cyber warfare poses unique challenges to global security, necessitating proactive measures to prevent cyber conflicts and attacks.

Robust cybersecurity practices are essential for protecting critical infrastructure and ensuring the safety and integrity of digital systems. Cybersecurity awareness and education empower individuals and organizations to become active contributors to a cyber-resilient society.

International cooperation is paramount in addressing cyber threats effectively. Collaboration among nations, the establishment of cyber norms, and the sharing of information are vital components of a collective approach to cybersecurity and peace.

As the cyber landscape continues to evolve, the significance of cybersecurity in preserving global peace will only grow. By embracing effective cybersecurity measures and fostering international cooperation, we can create a safer and more secure digital world, contributing to lasting peace and stability for generations to come.

PART 11:
THE ROLE OF RELIGIOUS AND SPIRITUAL LEADERS IN PEACEBUILDING

CHAPTER 23: INTERFAITH DIALOGUE AND PEACE

In a world often rife with conflicts rooted in religious differences, interfaith dialogue stands as a powerful tool for fostering understanding, tolerance, and peace. This chapter explores the significance of interfaith dialogue in promoting harmony, the pivotal role of religious and spiritual leaders in peacebuilding efforts, and the impact of successful interfaith initiatives in conflict resolution.

**The Significance of Interfaith Dialogue in Promoting Understanding and Tolerance: **

Interfaith dialogue serves as a bridge of understanding between individuals of different religious beliefs, fostering mutual respect and appreciation for diversity. By engaging in meaningful conversations, followers of various faiths can dismantle misconceptions and stereotypes that often fuel hostility and violence.

Through interfaith dialogue, people come to realize that despite different rituals and traditions, the underlying values of compassion, forgiveness, and love are universal across religions. This realization helps build empathy and trust among individuals from various faith backgrounds, laying the groundwork for peaceful coexistence.

**The Role of Religious and Spiritual Leaders in Peacebuilding Efforts: **

Religious and spiritual leaders play a crucial role as advocates for peace and harmony within their respective communities. They have the unique ability to influence attitudes and behaviours, and their moral authority can be harnessed to promote reconciliation and conflict resolution.

By using their positions to advocate for nonviolence and dialogue, religious leaders can inspire their followers to embrace peace and reject violence. Their involvement in peacebuilding efforts helps create a culture of tolerance and respect for diversity, which is essential for mitigating conflicts rooted in religious differences.

**Case Studies of Successful Interfaith Initiatives in Conflict Resolution: **

Throughout history, numerous interfaith initiatives have demonstrated the power of dialogue in resolving conflicts and promoting peace. One such example is the "Golden Temple of Amritsar" initiative in India, where Sikh, Hindu, and Muslim leaders came together to foster unity and understanding among their followers. This collaboration played a significant role in defusing religious tensions and promoting communal harmony.

Another case study is the "Religions for Peace" movement, an international organization that brings together religious leaders from different faith traditions to address pressing global challenges. The movement has contributed to peacebuilding efforts in conflict zones and facilitated dialogues aimed at overcoming religious divisions.

**Conclusion: **

Interfaith dialogue stands as a beacon of hope in a world plagued by religious conflicts. By promoting understanding and tolerance, it has the potential to build bridges between communities, transcend religious boundaries, and foster lasting peace.

Religious and spiritual leaders, with their moral authority, can be instrumental in inspiring their followers to embrace peace and reject violence. Their involvement in peacebuilding efforts is a testament to the unifying power of faith in promoting reconciliation.

The success of various interfaith initiatives, such as the "Golden Temple of Amritsar" and "Religions for Peace," further demonstrates the transformative potential of dialogue in resolving conflicts and building a more harmonious world.

As we move forward in our pursuit of peace, interfaith dialogue must continue to be nurtured and championed by individuals, communities, and nations alike. By embracing the principles of understanding, empathy, and respect for diversity, we can foster a global culture of peace, paving the way for a more compassionate and united world.

CHAPTER 24: RELIGIOUS EXTREMISM AND PEACEBUILDING

Religious extremism has emerged as a formidable challenge in today's world, contributing to the escalation of conflicts and hindering efforts to maintain peace. In this chapter, we delve into the complexities of religious extremism, explore strategies for countering its influence, and emphasize the significance of inclusive approaches in bridging religious divides for the sake of lasting peace.

**The Challenges of Religious Extremism in Fuelling Conflicts: **

Religious extremism occurs when individuals or groups interpret religious beliefs in an absolutist and radical manner, often justifying violence and intolerance towards those who do not share their views. In recent years, acts of terrorism and violence perpetrated in the name of religion have caused immense suffering and destabilized regions across the globe.

The influence of religious extremism can fuel pre-existing conflicts or instigate new ones, as adherents become increasingly isolated from other communities and governments. The oversimplification of complex issues and the demonization of perceived adversaries further exacerbate tensions, making it challenging to find common ground for peaceful resolutions.

**Strategies for Countering Religious Extremism and Promoting Peace: **

Addressing religious extremism requires a multifaceted approach that involves governments, civil society, religious leaders, and the international community. Here are some strategies to consider:

1. **Education and Awareness: ** Promoting education that fosters critical thinking, tolerance, and respect for diversity is essential in countering extremism. By encouraging dialogue about different belief systems and worldviews, individuals can develop a broader understanding of religious differences and find common values that unite them.

2. **Interfaith Dialogue: ** Engaging in interfaith

dialogue allows people from diverse religious backgrounds to come together and explore shared values. Such exchanges facilitate understanding, build bridges of empathy, and contribute to breaking down stereotypes and prejudices.

3. **Youth Engagement: ** Investing in the empowerment and engagement of young people can play a pivotal role in preventing radicalization. Providing youth with opportunities for education, employment, and social inclusion can help steer them away from extremist ideologies.

4. **Promoting Religious Leadership: ** Religious leaders have the potential to guide their communities away from extremism and towards peaceful coexistence. Empowering these leaders to preach messages of tolerance and respect can have a significant impact on countering extremist narratives.

5. **Media Literacy: ** Promoting media literacy can help individuals discern fact from fiction, reducing susceptibility to extremist propaganda. Encouraging responsible media reporting and discouraging sensationalism can also play a role in countering extremism.

**The Importance of Inclusive Approaches in Addressing Religious Divides: **

Inclusive approaches to peacebuilding are crucial for bridging religious divides and fostering social cohesion. It is essential to involve all segments of society in dialogue and decision-making processes, ensuring that diverse perspectives are heard and respected.

Exclusion and discrimination based on religious beliefs only perpetuate grievances and deepen divisions. In contrast, inclusive governance and policies can foster a sense of belonging and ownership, encouraging communities to work together towards common goals.

**Conclusion: **

Countering religious extremism and promoting peace requires a comprehensive and collaborative effort from all sectors of society. By addressing the root causes of extremism, engaging in dialogue, empowering religious leaders, and promoting inclusivity, we can create an environment conducive to sustainable peace.

Building a future free from the destructive influence of religious extremism requires nurturing mutual understanding, respect, and empathy. By fostering an environment where diverse religious beliefs are recognized and valued, we can lay the groundwork for a more peaceful and harmonious world. Only through concerted and compassionate action can we truly achieve the goal of keeping the peace and preventing the devastating consequences of wars fuelled by religious extremism.

PART 12: ENVIRONMENTAL STEWARDSHIP FOR PEACE

CHAPTER 25: ENVIRONMENTAL DEGRADATION AND CONFLICT

Environmental degradation has emerged as a significant catalyst for conflicts in the contemporary world. As the degradation of natural resources intensifies, competition for limited resources escalates, leading to tension, violence, and instability. In this chapter, we explore the complex relationship between environmental degradation and conflicts, emphasize the role of environmental stewardship in preventing resource-based conflicts, and shed light on the potential for environmental cooperation as a pathway to peace.

**The Link between Environmental Degradation and Conflicts: **

Environmental degradation, such as

deforestation, water scarcity, soil erosion, and climate change, can have dire consequences for communities and nations alike. These challenges not only threaten livelihoods but also fuel social and political unrest. When resources become scarce, disputes over access and control can arise, leading to tensions and conflicts between different groups.

In regions where natural resources are scarce or rapidly depleting, communities may resort to violence and armed conflict as a means of survival. Additionally, environmental degradation can exacerbate existing conflicts, as warring parties compete for dwindling resources and use them as bargaining chips in negotiations.

**The Role of Environmental Stewardship in Preventing Resource-Based Conflicts: **

Addressing environmental degradation is essential for preventing resource-based conflicts. Environmental stewardship involves responsibly managing and preserving natural resources to ensure their availability for present and future generations. Several strategies can be employed to promote environmental stewardship and reduce the risk of conflicts:

1. **Sustainable Resource Management: ** Implementing sustainable practices, such as reforestation, water conservation, and soil protection, can help mitigate the impact of

environmental degradation. Sustainable resource management ensures that resources are utilized in a manner that meets present needs without compromising future generations' ability to meet their needs.

2. **Community Engagement: ** Involving local communities in decision-making processes related to resource management is crucial. Empowering communities to have a say in how resources are utilized and ensuring equitable distribution can foster a sense of ownership and reduce the likelihood of conflicts.

3. **Environmental Policies and Regulations: ** Governments play a crucial role in enforcing environmental policies and regulations. Robust laws and mechanisms that address illegal resource extraction and promote responsible resource use are essential for preventing conflicts.

**The Potential for Environmental Cooperation as a Pathway to Peace: **

While environmental degradation can exacerbate conflicts, it also presents an opportunity for cooperation and peacebuilding. Recognizing the interdependence of nations on shared resources, environmental cooperation can foster dialogue and collaboration among countries, even during political tensions. Key factors for successful environmental cooperation include:

1. **Transboundary Cooperation: ** Many environmental challenges transcend national borders. By collaborating on transboundary issues like water management and air pollution, countries can build trust and establish channels for communication.

2. **Shared Environmental Goals: ** Identifying and working towards shared environmental goals can create common ground for cooperation. Collective efforts to combat climate change, protect biodiversity, and ensure sustainable resource use can pave the way for peacebuilding.

3. **Environmental Diplomacy: ** Environmental issues can provide a neutral platform for dialogue between nations. Environmental diplomacy seeks to find mutually beneficial solutions to environmental challenges, fostering relationships that extend beyond environmental cooperation.

**Conclusion: **

Environmental degradation poses a serious threat to global peace and security. However, it also presents an opportunity for collaboration and peacebuilding. By adopting responsible environmental stewardship, engaging communities, and fostering environmental cooperation, we can take significant strides towards preventing resource-based conflicts and creating a more sustainable and peaceful world.

Recognizing the intricate connection between environmental well-being and human security, the international community must come together to address environmental challenges with urgency and resolve. Only through collective action and commitment to environmental peacebuilding can we hope to stop wars and keep the peace.

CHAPTER 26: CLIMATE CHANGE AND PEACEBUILDING

Climate change has emerged as one of the most pressing challenges of our time, with far-reaching implications for global security and peace. In this chapter, we explore the profound impact of climate change on the dynamics of conflicts, the urgency of climate action in preventing future wars, and the crucial role of international agreements and cooperation in addressing climate-related challenges.

**The Impact of Climate Change on Global Security and Peace: **

Climate change has disrupted weather patterns, intensified natural disasters, and altered ecosystems, posing significant risks to human societies, and exacerbating existing vulnerabilities. As the consequences of climate change unfold, they intersect with social, economic, and political factors, leading to complex security challenges:

1. **Resource Scarcity: ** Climate-induced changes, such as water scarcity and declining agricultural productivity, can create competition over limited resources, leading to conflicts between communities and nations.

2. **Mass Migration: ** Rising sea levels and extreme weather events can trigger mass migration, straining social systems and creating tensions between host communities and displaced populations.

3. **Vulnerable Communities: ** Climate change disproportionately affects vulnerable populations, exacerbating poverty and social inequalities, which can fuel social unrest and conflict.

**The Need for Climate Action to Prevent Future Conflicts: **

Addressing climate change is not only an environmental imperative but also a critical step in preventing future conflicts. Climate action offers several pathways to promote peace and stability:

1. **Mitigating Resource Conflicts: ** By investing in renewable energy and sustainable practices, nations can reduce dependency on finite

resources, minimizing the potential for resource-based conflicts.

2. **Building Climate Resilience: ** Strengthening climate resilience in vulnerable regions can help communities withstand the impacts of climate change, reducing the risk of conflicts and displacement.

3. **Supporting Green Economies: ** Transitioning to green economies can create new opportunities for employment and economic growth, reducing competition over scarce resources.

**The Role of International Agreements and Cooperation in Addressing Climate-Related Challenges: **

Climate change is a global issue that demands a collective response. International agreements and cooperation are vital in tackling climate-related challenges:

1. **The Paris Agreement: ** The Paris Agreement, adopted in 2015, represents a landmark global commitment to combat climate change. It aims to limit global warming to well below 2 degrees Celsius and strengthen countries' abilities to cope with climate impacts.

2. **Climate Diplomacy: ** Diplomatic efforts play a crucial role in fostering international cooperation on climate change. Climate diplomacy seeks to bridge gaps between nations and forge consensus

on climate action.

3. **Climate Finance: ** Adequate climate finance is essential to support developing nations in their climate adaptation and mitigation efforts. Developed countries must fulfil their commitments to provide financial assistance to vulnerable nations.

**Conclusion: **

Climate change is a formidable challenge that intersects with global security and peace. As the world faces the consequences of a warming planet, the urgency of climate action cannot be overstated. Preventing future conflicts requires a concerted effort to address the root causes of climate change and build resilience in vulnerable communities. International cooperation and agreements play a crucial role in facilitating climate action and fostering peacebuilding efforts. By coming together to tackle the complex challenges of climate change, the international community can pave the way for a more sustainable and peaceful future. Embracing climate action to stop wars and keep the peace is not only a moral imperative but a strategic necessity for the well-being of current and future generations.

PART 13: ECONOMIC DEVELOPMENT AND PEACE

CHAPTER 27: ECONOMIC INEQUALITY AND CONFLICT

Economic inequality has long been recognized as a significant driver of social unrest and conflicts around the world. In this chapter, we delve into the intricate relationship between economic inequality and conflict, explore strategies for promoting economic development to prevent conflicts, and emphasize the crucial role of inclusive growth in maintaining peace.

**The Relationship Between Economic Inequality and Social Unrest: **

Economic inequality refers to the unequal distribution of wealth, resources, and opportunities within a society. When this inequality becomes extreme, it can lead to various forms of social unrest and conflict:

1. **Social Discontent: ** Economic disparities can foster feelings of resentment and disillusionment among marginalized communities, leading to social discontent and protests.

2. **Political Instability: ** High levels of economic inequality can erode trust in institutions and exacerbate political instability, making societies more susceptible to conflicts.

3. **Crime and Violence: ** Economic disparities can fuel criminal activities as individuals seek to escape poverty or exploit others' vulnerabilities.

**Strategies for Promoting Economic Development to Prevent Conflicts: **

Promoting economic development and reducing economic inequality are essential steps in preventing conflicts and promoting peace:

1. **Investing in Education: ** Providing quality education to all citizens can break the cycle of poverty and empower individuals with the skills and knowledge needed to participate in the economy.

2. **Creating Job Opportunities: ** Encouraging entrepreneurship, supporting small and medium-sized enterprises, and attracting foreign investments can create job opportunities and spur economic growth.

3. **Social Safety Nets: ** Implementing social safety net programs, such as unemployment benefits and cash transfers, can provide a safety net for vulnerable populations and alleviate economic hardships.

**The Importance of Inclusive Growth in Maintaining Peace: **

Inclusive growth, which ensures that the benefits of economic development are distributed equitably across society, is a crucial component of maintaining peace:

1. **Social Cohesion: ** Inclusive growth fosters social cohesion by reducing economic disparities and promoting a sense of shared prosperity among citizens.

2. **Political Stability: ** When economic growth benefits all segments of society, it enhances political stability and reduces the potential for conflicts over resource distribution.

3. **Addressing Root Causes of Conflict: ** Inclusive growth addresses the root causes of conflicts by creating opportunities for marginalized groups and reducing feelings of alienation and exclusion.

**Conclusion: **

Economic inequality has far-reaching implications for social stability and peace.

Recognizing the relationship between economic disparities and conflicts is essential in developing effective strategies for conflict prevention. By promoting economic development, investing in education, and fostering inclusive growth, societies can create an environment where peace can flourish. Governments, international organizations, and civil society must work together to address economic inequality and prioritize policies that uplift vulnerable populations and promote shared prosperity. Only by fostering a more equitable and inclusive world can we effectively stop wars and keep the peace for generations to come.

CHAPTER 28: BUSINESS AND PEACE

In recent years, there has been a growing recognition of the significant role that businesses can play in promoting peace and stability in conflict zones. This chapter explores the multifaceted relationship between businesses and peace, delves into the concept of corporate social responsibility (CSR), and highlights case studies of businesses contributing to peace and stability in their operations.

**The Role of Businesses in Conflict Zones and Peacebuilding Efforts: **

Businesses can have both positive and negative impacts on peace in conflict-affected regions:

1. **Economic Stability: ** In conflict zones, businesses can provide employment opportunities and contribute to economic stability, reducing the desperation that often fuels

violence and unrest.

2. **Resource Management: ** Responsible resource management by businesses can help prevent conflicts arising from disputes over valuable resources.

3. **Conflict Sensitivity: ** Businesses need to be aware of the potential risks of operating in conflict zones and ensure their activities do not exacerbate existing tensions.

**Corporate Social Responsibility and Its Impact on Peace: **

Corporate Social Responsibility (CSR) refers to businesses' commitment to operating ethically and contributing positively to society. In the context of peace, CSR can have significant impacts:

1. **Community Engagement: ** Businesses can engage with local communities, listening to their concerns and actively involving them in decision-making processes. This approach fosters a sense of ownership and reduces the likelihood of conflicts arising due to grievances.

2. **Conflict Sensitivity Training: ** Training employees to be conflict-sensitive allows businesses to operate with awareness of potential conflicts and respond responsibly when challenges arise.

3. **Promoting Social Inclusion: ** Emphasizing

diversity and inclusivity in the workplace can contribute to social cohesion and harmony within communities.

**Case Studies of Businesses Contributing to Peace and Stability: **

Several businesses have demonstrated their commitment to peace and social impact through their practices:

1. **Levi Strauss & Co.**: This global apparel company has collaborated with local organizations to address social issues and promote peacebuilding efforts in regions affected by conflict.

2. **Nestlé**: The company has established initiatives that focus on sustainable agricultural practices and community development, contributing to stability and economic growth in rural areas.

3. **Siemens**: As part of its CSR efforts, Siemens has invested in educational programs in conflict-affected regions, aiming to provide young people with opportunities for personal and professional development.

**Conclusion: **

The private sector has a critical role to play in promoting peace and stability in conflict zones. Businesses can leverage their resources, influence, and expertise to create positive social impact and contribute to peacebuilding efforts. By adopting responsible business practices, engaging with local communities, and prioritizing corporate social responsibility, businesses can become valuable partners in efforts to stop wars and keep the peace. Governments, civil society, and international organizations must collaborate with businesses to encourage responsible business practices and harness the private sector's potential for advancing peace around the world.

PART 14: THE GLOBAL EFFORT FOR PEACE

CHAPTER 29: INTERNATIONAL COOPERATION FOR PEACE

In an increasingly interconnected world, international cooperation is paramount for maintaining peace and resolving conflicts effectively. This chapter explores the significance of multilateralism in conflict resolution, the pivotal role of international organizations and alliances in keeping the peace, and the challenges and opportunities in global peace efforts.

**The Significance of Multilateralism in Conflict Resolution: **

Multilateralism refers to the cooperation and collaboration between multiple nations and international organizations to address global challenges, including conflicts. It plays a crucial role in conflict resolution for the following reasons:

1. **Collective Decision-making: ** Multilateral approaches allow nations to collectively decide on solutions to conflicts, ensuring a more inclusive and diverse range of perspectives.

2. **Leveraging Resources: ** By pooling together resources and expertise, countries can address conflicts with greater efficiency and effectiveness.

3. **Building Trust: ** Multilateralism fosters trust and understanding among nations, reducing the likelihood of misunderstandings and miscalculations that could escalate tensions.

**The Role of International Organizations and Alliances in Maintaining Peace: **

1. **United Nations (UN): ** The United Nations is a central player in international peace efforts, deploying peacekeeping missions, facilitating diplomatic negotiations, and providing humanitarian aid in conflict-affected regions.

2. **North Atlantic Treaty Organization (NATO): ** NATO is a military alliance that plays a vital role in deterring conflicts and promoting stability among its member states.

3. **African Union (AU): ** The AU is actively involved in peacekeeping and conflict resolution efforts within Africa, providing regional solutions to regional challenges.

**The Challenges and Opportunities in Global Peace Efforts: **

1. **Political Divides: ** Differing political interests among nations can hinder effective cooperation in conflict resolution, leading to inaction and prolonged conflicts.

2. **Resource Constraints: ** Limited resources may impede the ability of international organizations to respond swiftly and adequately to conflicts.

3. **Regional Specificities: ** Conflicts often have unique regional characteristics, requiring tailor-made solutions and comprehensive understanding of local dynamics.

**Opportunities for Global Peace Efforts: **

1. **Diplomatic Dialogue: ** Diplomatic channels offer opportunities for peaceful dialogue and negotiations to de-escalate conflicts.

2. **Early Warning Mechanisms: ** Investing in early warning systems can help anticipate and prevent potential conflicts before they escalate.

3. **Preventive Diplomacy: ** By addressing root causes and triggers of conflicts, preventive diplomacy can contribute to long-term peacebuilding.

**Conclusion: **

International cooperation is a linchpin in the efforts to stop wars and maintain peace. Multilateralism ensures that nations work together, leveraging collective wisdom and resources for effective conflict resolution. International organizations and alliances, such as the United Nations, NATO, and the African Union, play crucial roles in peacekeeping, diplomacy, and humanitarian aid. While challenges exist, opportunities for global peace efforts are abundant, including diplomatic dialogue, early warning mechanisms, and preventive diplomacy. As nations continue to navigate complex geopolitical landscapes, fostering international cooperation will remain indispensable in promoting a peaceful and harmonious world. The collective commitment of countries and international organizations is essential in realizing a future free from conflicts and wars.

CHAPTER 30: PEACEBUILDING IN THE 21ST CENTURY

As the world continues to evolve, conflicts and peacebuilding efforts have also undergone significant transformations. This chapter delves into the changing nature of conflicts and peacebuilding in the 21st century, explores strategies for adapting to the dynamic global landscape, and highlights the crucial role of new technologies and innovative approaches in advancing peace.

**The Evolving Nature of Conflicts and Peacebuilding: **

1. **Complexity of Conflicts: ** Conflicts in the 21st century is often characterized by multifaceted drivers, involving a combination of political, economic, social, and environmental factors.

2. **Non-State Actors: ** The rise of non-state actors, such as terrorist organizations and armed militias, has added complexity to conflicts, challenging traditional peacebuilding approaches.

3. **Transnational Conflicts: ** Conflicts today often transcend borders, requiring international collaboration and cooperation in peacebuilding efforts.

**Strategies for Adapting Peacebuilding Efforts: **

1. **Inclusive Approaches: ** Inclusive peacebuilding, involving all relevant stakeholders, is essential for sustainable and lasting solutions to conflicts.

2. **Conflict Sensitivity: ** Adopting conflict-sensitive approaches ensures that interventions do not inadvertently exacerbate tensions or contribute to violence.

3. **Gender Mainstreaming: ** Integrating gender perspectives in peacebuilding efforts acknowledges the unique experiences of men, women, and gender-diverse individuals in conflicts.

**The Role of New Technologies and Innovative Approaches: **

1. **Digital Diplomacy: ** social media and digital platforms offer new avenues for diplomatic

engagement and public outreach in peacebuilding.

2. **Data Analytics: ** Utilizing big data and analytics can enhance early warning systems and facilitate evidence-based decision-making in conflict prevention.

3. **Virtual Reality (VR): ** VR technology can be employed to enhance empathy and understanding among conflicting parties, fostering reconciliation.

**Harnessing Youth and Women: ** Engaging youth and women in peacebuilding efforts empowers marginalized voices and promotes intergenerational collaboration in shaping peaceful societies.

**Sustainable Development Goals (SDGs): ** Aligning peacebuilding initiatives with the SDGs fosters comprehensive and integrated approaches to addressing the root causes of conflicts.

**Technological Advancements in Conflict Resolution: **

1. **Conflict Mapping: ** Geographic Information Systems (GIS) enable detailed conflict mapping, enhancing situational awareness for peacebuilders.

2. **Early Warning Systems: ** Advanced algorithms and data analytics enhance early warning systems, allowing for timely responses to

potential conflicts.

3. **Blockchain for Peace: ** Blockchain technology can increase transparency and accountability in peacebuilding initiatives, ensuring efficient resource allocation.

**Innovative Approaches to Mediation and Negotiation: **

1. **Track II Diplomacy: ** Track II diplomacy involves non-governmental actors and informal channels to facilitate dialogue and bridge divides.

2. **Citizen Diplomacy: ** Engaging civil society and grassroots organizations in peace negotiations fosters bottom-up peacebuilding efforts.

3. **Arts and Culture: ** Leveraging arts and culture as mediums for peacebuilding can promote dialogue, healing, and reconciliation among conflicting communities.

**Conclusion: **

In the 21st century, peacebuilding efforts have evolved to meet the complexities of modern conflicts. Adapting to the dynamic global landscape requires inclusive, conflict-sensitive, and gender-responsive approaches. Embracing new technologies and innovative practices can enhance the effectiveness and efficiency of peacebuilding initiatives. Digital diplomacy, data analytics, virtual reality, and other technological advancements provide valuable tools for conflict resolution and reconciliation.

Moreover, involving youth, women, and marginalized groups, as well as aligning peacebuilding efforts with the Sustainable Development Goals, strengthens the foundation for lasting peace. By harnessing the power of technology and innovation, and engaging diverse actors in peacebuilding, the world can make strides toward preventing conflicts and building a more peaceful and harmonious future. Embracing these 21st-century strategies and approaches will pave the way for a world that prioritizes dialogue, cooperation, and understanding over violence and hostility.

PART 15: THE INDIVIDUAL'S ROLE IN PROMOTING PEACE

CHAPTER 31: EVERYDAY PEACEBUILDING

Peacebuilding is not solely the domain of diplomats and world leaders; it is a responsibility that each individual carry within them. In Chapter 31, we explore the significance of everyday peacebuilding and the transformative impact of individual actions in promoting peace in our daily lives.

**The Power of Individual Actions: **

1. **The Butterfly Effect: ** Just as a butterfly's wings can create a tornado on the other side of the world, small acts of kindness, compassion, and understanding can ripple outwards, positively affecting others.

2. **Breaking the Cycle: ** Individuals who choose to respond to conflicts with non-violence and understanding can disrupt the cycle of hostility and retaliation.

3. **Leading by Example: ** By embodying peaceful attitudes and behaviours, individuals can inspire others to follow suit, fostering a culture of peace within their communities.

**The Importance of Empathy, Compassion, and Active Listening: **

1. **Empathy: ** Empathy is the cornerstone of conflict resolution, allowing individuals to understand and connect with the experiences and emotions of others.

2. **Compassion: ** Compassion drives individuals to take action to alleviate the suffering of others, fostering an environment of support and care.

3. **Active Listening: ** Listening actively and attentively to the concerns and perspectives of others builds trust and opens pathways for dialogue and resolution.

**The Ripple Effect of Small Acts of Peacebuilding: **

1. **Creating Safe Spaces: ** By creating safe and empathetic spaces for dialogue, individuals can encourage open communication and understanding.

2. **Resolving Personal Conflicts: ** Addressing personal conflicts with empathy and compassion can have a positive influence on resolving larger

societal conflicts.

3. **Supporting Social Justice: ** Advocating for social justice issues, such as poverty reduction and human rights, contributes to a more equitable and peaceful world.

**Promoting Peace in Daily Life: **

1. **Cultivating Inner Peace: ** Practicing self-reflection, mindfulness, and self-care enables individuals to approach conflicts with a clear and cantered mind.

2. **Promoting Diversity and Inclusion: ** Embracing diversity and promoting inclusion fosters harmony and appreciation for different perspectives.

3. **Choosing Non-Violent Communication: ** By opting for non-violent and constructive communication, individuals can de-escalate tensions and resolve conflicts peacefully.

**Peacebuilding in Communities: **

1. **Community Service and Volunteerism: ** Engaging in community service and volunteer work fosters a sense of belonging and solidarity within communities.

2. **Conflict Resolution Workshops: ** Participating in conflict resolution workshops equips individuals with essential skills to navigate

disputes peacefully.

3. **Promoting Education and Awareness:** ** Spreading knowledge about peacebuilding, conflict resolution, and human rights encourages collective efforts for a peaceful world.

**Conclusion: **

In the pursuit of global peace, it is crucial to recognize the power of individual actions and everyday peacebuilding. Each person has the potential to contribute to a more peaceful world through acts of kindness, empathy, and compassion. By cultivating inner peace, promoting understanding, and choosing non-violent communication, we create ripples of positive change that extend beyond ourselves.

Moreover, in communities, everyday peacebuilding is achieved through community service, conflict resolution workshops, and educational initiatives. By embracing diversity, promoting inclusion, and advocating for social justice, we can build more harmonious societies.

The world needs individuals committed to being agents of peace, and by doing so, they become catalysts for a collective transformation. Each act of peacebuilding, no matter how small, matters, and collectively, these efforts can create a profound impact on the world. As we reflect on our own capacity for peacebuilding, we realize that peace is not an abstract concept; it is a way of life that begins with us. Let us embrace the potential of everyday peacebuilding and work together to create a world where conflicts are resolved through empathy, understanding, and peaceful dialogue.

CHAPTER 32: EDUCATION FOR PEACE

Education is a powerful tool in shaping societies and individuals. In Chapter 32, we delve into the essential role of education in fostering a culture of peace, exploring peace education programs and initiatives worldwide, and understanding its potential to break the cycle of violence and promote understanding.

**The Role of Education in Fostering a Culture of Peace: **

1. **Building Empathy and Understanding: ** Peace education cultivates empathy, encouraging individuals to understand the experiences and perspectives of others, ultimately fostering tolerance and respect.

2. **Promoting Critical Thinking: ** By encouraging critical thinking skills, education enables individuals to analyse conflicts and seek

non-violent resolutions.

3. **Nurturing Conflict Resolution Skills: ** Peace education equips individuals with effective conflict resolution strategies, empowering them to address disputes constructively.

**Peace Education Programs and Initiatives Worldwide: **

1. **United Nations Educational, Scientific, and Cultural Organization (UNESCO): ** UNESCO actively promotes peace education through its initiatives, advocating for curriculum reforms that incorporate peacebuilding and human rights education.

2. **The Peace Education Initiative by Peace Direct: ** This organization works to promote peace education in areas affected by conflicts, empowering local communities to build peace from within.

3. **The Global Campaign for Peace Education (GCPE): ** GCPE is a collective of organizations and individuals committed to advancing peace education globally, advocating for its inclusion in educational systems.

**The Potential of Education in Breaking the Cycle of Violence: **

1. **Addressing Root Causes of Conflicts: ** By educating individuals about the root causes of

conflicts, education helps prevent violence at its source.

2. **Promoting Social and Emotional Learning: ** Education that focuses on social and emotional learning equips students with vital skills to navigate emotions, communicate effectively, and build positive relationships, reducing the likelihood of aggressive behaviour.

3. **Encouraging Global Citizenship: ** Education can foster a sense of global citizenship, encouraging individuals to view themselves as part of a broader, interconnected world, promoting peace and understanding across borders.

**Promoting Understanding and Peaceful Coexistence: **

1. **Cultural and Religious Awareness: ** Education helps students appreciate cultural and religious diversity, fostering an environment of mutual respect and peaceful coexistence.

2. **Conflict Analysis and Resolution: ** Peace education includes teaching students how to analyse conflicts and explore peaceful resolutions, preparing them to become active agents of change in their communities.

3. **Engaging Youth in Peacebuilding: ** By empowering young minds with peace education, we empower the next generation to be proactive

peacebuilders and advocates for positive change.

**The Role of Teachers in Peace Education: **

1. **Role Models for Peace: ** Teachers play a vital role as role models for peace, demonstrating the values of empathy, tolerance, and respect in their classrooms.

2. **Creating Safe Spaces: ** Educators create safe spaces for students to discuss conflicts and challenging topics openly, fostering an environment of trust and understanding.

3. **Empowering Students' Voices: ** Teachers encourage students to voice their opinions and ideas on peace and conflict, empowering them to be active participants in peacebuilding efforts.

**Conclusion: **

Education for peace is not only about providing information but also about nurturing values, skills, and attitudes that promote peaceful coexistence and conflict resolution. By incorporating peace education into curricula, we can empower individuals with the tools to break the cycle of violence and build a more compassionate and harmonious world.

Through peace education programs and initiatives worldwide, we witness the transformative power of education in promoting understanding, empathy, and global citizenship. Teachers play a crucial role in this endeavour, guiding students to become proactive peacebuilders and agents of change.

As we embrace the potential of education for peace, we recognize that investing in the education of our youth is an investment in a future built on cooperation, compassion, and respect. Education holds the key to transforming conflicts, promoting understanding, and fostering a culture of peace that can resonate across generations. By nurturing the seeds of peace within our educational systems, we sow the seeds of a more peaceful and just world for all.

PART 16: LESSONS FROM HISTORY

CHAPTER 33: THE LESSONS OF PAST CONFLICTS

As we continue our journey in understanding how to stop wars and keep the peace, Chapter 33 delves into the invaluable insights gained from historical case studies of successful conflict resolution and peacebuilding efforts. This chapter highlights the lessons learned from past mistakes and failures in preventing wars, emphasizing the significance of historical knowledge in shaping future peace strategies.

**Historical Case Studies of Successful Conflict Resolution: **

1. **The End of Apartheid in South Africa: ** The peaceful transition from apartheid to democracy in South Africa, spearheaded by leaders like Nelson Mandela, demonstrated the power of reconciliation and negotiation in resolving deep-rooted conflicts.

2. **The Peaceful Revolution in Czechoslovakia:** The Velvet Revolution in 1989 showcased the effectiveness of non-violent resistance in achieving political change, ultimately leading to the dissolution of the Communist regime.

3. **The Dayton Agreement in Bosnia and Herzegovina:** The 1995 Dayton Agreement brought an end to the Bosnian War, illustrating the significance of international mediation and peace negotiations in complex conflicts.

The Lessons Learned from Past Mistakes and Failures:

1. **The Consequences of Ignoring Early Warning Signs:** Many conflicts throughout history could have been prevented if early warning signs had been recognized and addressed. Failing to act on these warnings can lead to the escalation of tensions and violence.

2. **The Importance of Inclusivity:** Peace efforts that exclude certain groups or communities often lead to incomplete or unsustainable solutions. Inclusive dialogue and participation of all stakeholders are essential for lasting peace.

3. **The Dangers of Imposing Solutions:** Attempts to impose one-sided solutions on conflicting parties often lead to resentment and future tensions. Instead, negotiated settlements that respect the interests of all parties have a

higher chance of success.

**The Significance of Historical Knowledge in Shaping Future Peace Strategies: **

1. **Building on Successful Models: ** By studying successful case studies, we can identify patterns and strategies that have proven effective in resolving conflicts. These models can serve as blueprints for future peacebuilding efforts.

2. **Learning from Past Mistakes: ** Understanding the failures of past peace efforts helps us avoid repeating the same mistakes and adopt more effective approaches.

3. **Applying Contextual Knowledge: ** Historical knowledge provides valuable context for current conflicts, helping us recognize underlying dynamics and potential pitfalls.

**Promoting Peace through Historical Education: **

1. **Teaching History with a Peacebuilding Lens: ** Integrating peacebuilding perspectives into history curricula can help students develop critical thinking skills and a deeper understanding of the causes and consequences of conflicts.

2. **Encouraging Dialogue and Reflection: ** Educators can facilitate discussions and reflections on historical conflicts, encouraging students to explore alternative outcomes and

consider the impact of different strategies.

3. **Drawing Inspiration from Peace Heroes: ** Highlighting the contributions of peace heroes from history can inspire young minds to be proactive peacebuilders in their communities.

**Conclusion: **

History has taught us that peace is achievable through proactive efforts, inclusivity, and the willingness to learn from past experiences. By studying historical case studies of successful conflict resolution and reflecting on past mistakes, we gain valuable insights into how to build a more peaceful future.

In a world where conflicts persist, the significance of historical knowledge in shaping future peace strategies cannot be overstated. By integrating peacebuilding perspectives into history education, we empower the next generation with the knowledge and tools to contribute to a more peaceful and just world.

As we move forward on the path of keeping the peace, let us draw inspiration from the successes of the past and embrace the lessons learned from history. By doing so, we can work together to create a future where wars are but distant memories, replaced by a world united in its pursuit of peace and understanding.

CHAPTER 34: THE JOURNEY AHEAD

As we near the conclusion of this book, "How to Stop Wars: Keeping the Peace," we find ourselves reflecting on the profound exploration of conflict, peace, and war that has filled its pages. Throughout our journey, we have encountered the complexities of human interactions, the causes and consequences of conflicts, and the strategies employed to achieve peace. We have learned that peace is not merely the absence of war but a dynamic and continuous process that requires active engagement and commitment from all of us.

Our exploration of various conflict resolution theories, diplomatic efforts, and peacebuilding initiatives has taught us that the path to peace is not always easy, but it is essential. It calls for understanding, empathy, and a willingness to see beyond differences. We have learned that preventing conflicts is far preferable than resolving them, and this requires addressing root causes, promoting inclusive growth, and advocating for human rights.

In Chapter 33, we discovered the lessons of past conflicts, drawing insights from historical case studies that exemplify successful peacebuilding efforts. History has taught us that peace is possible, even in the most challenging of circumstances, through dialogue, negotiation, and a commitment to finding common ground.

We have also delved into the power of individuals and communities in Chapter 31, recognizing that peacebuilding is not solely the responsibility of governments or international organizations. Each one of us can contribute to peace through everyday actions of kindness, understanding, and compassion. By promoting peace in our daily lives and advocating for peaceful solutions to conflicts, we can create a ripple effect that extends beyond borders.

As we look towards the journey ahead, we are reminded of the immense challenges that lie ahead in achieving a more peaceful world. Conflict continues to be a reality for far too many people, and the consequences of war are felt deeply by individuals, families, and entire communities. But we are also filled with hope, knowing that each step towards peace, no matter how small, matters.

We extend a call to action to every reader of this book - to stand up against violence, to advocate for peaceful resolutions, and to foster an environment of dialogue and understanding. We believe that peace is not an unattainable dream but a tangible reality that can be achieved through collective efforts.

We urge governments, policymakers, and international organizations to prioritize peacebuilding and conflict prevention in their agendas. Investing in education, promoting economic development, and addressing social inequalities are fundamental to building lasting peace.

To the young minds reading these words, we encourage you to be the changemakers of tomorrow. Embrace your capacity to contribute to peace, challenge the status quo, and promote dialogue and cooperation in your communities.

Finally, we envision a world where wars are replaced by negotiations, where conflicts are resolved through understanding, and where peace is not just a fleeting moment but an enduring reality. This vision can only be realized when we come together with empathy, respect, and a shared commitment to the common good.

As we bid farewell to this book, let us carry its wisdom in our hearts and minds. Let us embark on the journey ahead with determination and hope, knowing that together, we can make the world a more peaceful and harmonious place for generations to come.

The journey of peacebuilding is one that knows no end, but it is a journey worth taking. May we all find the courage to take the first step and continue walking hand in hand, united in our pursuit of peace. Together, let us keep the peace, for a better world is within our reach.

Conclusion: Embracing Peace as a Global Imperative

As we come to the end of this enlightening journey through "How to Stop Wars: Keeping the Peace," we find ourselves standing at a crossroads where the path to peace diverges from the road to conflict. Throughout the chapters, we have explored the intricate web of conflicts, the vital role of peacebuilding, and the power of human compassion. We have learned that peace is not a passive state but an active and continuous pursuit that requires collective effort and unwavering commitment.

In this concluding chapter, we revisit the key messages and themes that have emerged from our exploration. From understanding the complexities of conflict in Chapter 1 to embracing peace as a global responsibility in Chapter 34, we have witnessed the significance of peace in shaping our shared future.

In Chapter 1, we defined conflict as the convergence of divergent interests, ideologies, and values that often result in violence and hostility. The causes of conflicts are manifold, ranging from historical grievances to socio-economic inequalities, and they can impact individuals and societies in profound ways.

Throughout the chapters, we discovered a plethora of strategies for conflict prevention and resolution. From diplomatic negotiations and peacekeeping missions to grassroots efforts and interfaith dialogues, we learned that there is no one-size-fits-all approach to peacebuilding. Instead, a combination of these methods, tailored to each unique situation, can pave the way for lasting peace.

One recurring theme in our exploration has been the crucial role of education. In Chapter 32, we recognized that education is not only a means to acquire knowledge but also a powerful tool for cultivating a culture of peace. By teaching conflict resolution skills, promoting empathy, and fostering an understanding of diverse perspectives, we can equip the next generation with the tools they need to build a more peaceful world.

We also delved into the impact of environmental degradation, economic inequality, and religious extremism on conflicts. Chapter 25 highlighted the link between environmental depletion and resource-based conflicts, emphasizing the urgency of environmental stewardship. In Chapter 27, we acknowledged that economic inequality and social unrest often go hand in hand, underlining the importance of inclusive growth in peacebuilding. Furthermore, Chapter 24 revealed the challenges posed by religious extremism and the need for inclusive approaches to address religious divides.

As we explored the efforts of women as peacebuilders in Chapter 17 and the Women, Peace, and Security Agenda in Chapter 18, we were reminded of the transformative potential of gender equality in building sustainable peace. Their contributions have proven time and again that peace cannot thrive without the active participation of women in conflict resolution and peacebuilding processes.

In Chapter 30, we recognized the profound impact of technology and social media on peacebuilding efforts, amplifying both the potential for positive change and the challenges of misinformation and polarization. We must approach technological advancements with ethical considerations to harness their power for peace.

With each case study, theory, and insight, one resounding message echoes throughout this book: peace is not an abstract concept, but a living, breathing force that requires action and dedication from each one of us. As we conclude this journey, we call upon our readers to embrace peace as a global imperative.

Whether it is by advocating for policies that promote peace and equality, engaging in peaceful dialogue with those who hold different perspectives, or supporting organizations and initiatives dedicated to peacebuilding, every individual has the power to contribute to a more harmonious world.

Let us heed the call to action and take steps, big or small, in promoting peace in our communities and beyond. Let us challenge the notion that conflict is inevitable and embrace the belief that peace is achievable.

As we close the chapter on this book, may we carry its wisdom in our hearts and minds, and may it inspire us to keep the peace in all that we do. The road to peace may be long and challenging, but it is a journey worth taking. Together, hand in hand, let us work towards a world where wars are mere memories of the past, and peace flourishes in every corner of our planet. For it is in our collective efforts that we shall find the true meaning of peace - a world where compassion reigns, understanding prevails, and the pursuit of peace becomes our shared global imperative.